More That I Never Knew About COLORADO

ABBOTT FAY

WESTERN REFLECTIONS
PUBLISHING COMPANY

Library of Congress Cataloging Number 00 - 105540

ISBN 1-890437-54-9

Cover Design by SJS Design (Susan Smilanic)

Western Reflections Publishing Company

Box 710

Ouray, Colorado 81427

First Edition

TABLE OF CONTENTS

ABOUT INTERESTING PLACES

ABOUT QUESTIONABLE BEHAVIOR AND OUTRIGHT LAWLESSNESS

ABOUT DISASTROUS EVENTS

A SHORT NOTE OF EXPLANATION

The writer spent most of his career noting long-forgotten or little-publicized people, happenings, or places in Colorado. These he gathered into an earlier book entitled **I Never Knew That About Colorado.** It was quite amazing how many readers furnished him with additional items for that "quaint volume of forgotten lore."

Those, and more travel for research, brought forth these true stories, lest they be lost as a part of the great tradition of Colorado.

Abbott Fay

Grand Junction, Colorado

May, 2000

ABOUT INTERESTING PEOPLE

HE AMPUTATED HIS OWN LEG

It Happened in North Park

North Park, in Jackson County, is unique in its location at the headwaters of the North Platte River, which runs north into Wyoming and later joins the South Platte in Nebraska. It is isolated by mountains from both the eastern plains and the Western Slope.

In 1827, a party of trappers was hunting there when they were attacked by either Ute or Arapahoe Indians. Among the mountain men was Tom Smith. Smith had already made a name for himself, trapping in southeastern Colorado and having engaged in some fights with Indians, including at least one massacre of the natives about which he boasted.

Now he was twenty-six years old and was hit by an arrow which pierced his leg just above the ankle, splitting the bone. When he limped over to a nearby tree, the bone slipped out of his flesh onto the moist earth. There would have to be an amputation. None of the other members of the party had the heart to cut off his leg, so Smith took a butcher knife and did the job himself. One partner, Milton Sublette, did burn the stump to cauterize the wound after Smith had lost much of his blood. The men fashioned a stretcher and took him west to the Green River in northwestern Colorado, where he recovered after several months. They fashioned a wooden leg for him, and from that time on he was known as Pegleg Smith.

He learned to ride a horse skillfully with his new attachment and went on to become one of the greatest horse thieves in the history of the West, but he was never prosecuted. In 1829, along with some cohorts, he stole at least 300 horses in the Los Angeles area, selling them one by one. This was so successful that ten years later he joined up with a famous Ute Indian leader, Walkara, who had a small band of followers. Along with frontiersman Jim Beckwourth, they stole more than 3,000 horses in California.

Pegleg Smith later established a ranch near Bear Lake in northern Utah, where he sold stolen horses to immigrants on the Oregon and Mormon Trails. They followed the California gold rush of 1849, and he procured more livestock to sell to those wayfarers.

Eventually Smith joined the gold seekers and was reported to have found a rich lode in California. He never developed it for some reason, but searches after his death in 1866 for the mythical "Pegleg Smith gold" provided that state with another mining legend.

An early day trapper/hunter. Harper's Weekly, *September 9, 1876*

RATTLESNAKE JACK WAS A WOLF HUNTER

He was Never Known to Use Soap and Water

When the area around Walden, in North Park, was invaded by a wolf pack for the first time, the cattlemen offered a bounty of seventy-five dollars for each wolf killed. That was in the relatively mild winter of 1909-1910. They called in a man famous for his success in trapping wolves in Wyoming. He went by the name of Rattlesnake Jack. Rattlesnake got his name because he claimed to have handled the serpents in a carnival sideshow at one time, and also because he ate a lot of rattlesnake meat as well as skunks and muskrats.

The wolves had killed three horses and forty-eight cattle. At first, the losses were blamed on coyotes, who seem to have had a habit of following the wolves to clean up whatever was left after the killers had eaten their fill. When a wolf was finally spotted, the ranchers realized that only a professional wolf hunter could solve the problem.

It was said a person could smell Jack a quarter of a mile off, as he never was known to use soap and water. That, he claimed, was how he could lay traps without leaving any human smell which would drive the wolves away. Jack was also addicted to morphine, and the physician in Walden supplied him rather than have the man go insane.

Jack, whose last name seems to have been forgotten, brought along his son, a man who did perhaps bathe occasionally. He was called "Little Rattle" in spite of his large size.

His secret in trapping seems to have been a scent that he placed on dead carcasses. It was believed he made it from the droppings of a female wolf he had captured alive.

Bounty was paid only when four feet of hide and the scalp of a wolf were submitted. The total number of wolves killed came to about seven, and if others were in the pack, they left soon after Rattlesnake Jack did his work. After the trapper and his son and three dogs returned to Wyoming, there were no wolves left in North Park.

SILVER CLIFF'S SUCCESSFUL YOUTH COUNSELOR

Lew Key, Chinese Laundryman

Silver Cliff, about a mile from the town of Westcliff, in Custer County, was a booming mining camp in the 1880s. It was then that a young man, Lew Key, came from China to establish a laundry service for the town.

He had left his wife in China, expecting to send for her when he could afford to do so. Meantime he became very popular with the local citizenry, and was a teacher in the Presbyterian Sunday School. He developed a good rapport with the children and teenagers of the town.

As time went on, people began to regard Key as a wise man, bringing their problems to him. He was especially successful in straightening out problem adolescents. Sons and daughters who misbehaved were sent to the laundryman for counseling, and they all seemed to change their attitudes as a result of talks with Lew Key. Many went on to become highly respected citizens, always acknowledging the guidance given by this counselor.

He probably passed on much of the Oriental thought regarding filial piety and honor to parents, and imbued the youth with a broader perspective. In any event, it seems that almost every one who came to him brought home a sense of peace to the family, according to historian Gayle Turk.

It seems as though the laundryman wrote a letter to his wife every night, but would only mail the stack of letters once a year. He never did send for his wife.

By 1927, the town population had declined to only about twenty people, including Lew Key, who died that year and was buried there.

MANITOU'S FULL-SERVICE DOCTOR

From Prescription to Mummification

Dr. Isaac Davis arrived in Manitou Springs in 1871. He had won a medal in the Crimean War, came to America, and was wounded in the Civil War Battle of Bull Run. Then getting his medical certification, he worked at New York University Medical College, where he contracted the dreaded killer, tuberculosis.

Colorado was considered one of the best places for recovery from that "white death" sentence. Dr. Isaac found himself cured after only a short time of basking in the sun, getting plenty of rest, and partaking of the reportedly "healing waters" of Manitou.

Determined to help other sufferers, he often prescribed patent drugs. Then he established the first drug store in town to fill his own prescriptions. In case the patient did die, Davis was the County Coroner who verified the cause.

This innovative man was the town's only mortician for a long time, so he then did the embalming, and marketed the casket. Following a funeral, which was probably performed by somebody else, the interment was in the cemetery on Pawnee Avenue, which was owned and operated by Davis. When the town began to grow, Davis sold the Pawnee site and supervised the exhumations and reburials to the Crystal Valley cemetery.

Becoming impressed with his skill in mortuary arts, he set out to perform the ultimate achievement in that field: a perfect mummy. When a drunk named Tom O'Neal was killed in a gambling game, the body was brought to Dr. Davis. The doctor spent two years working with all his skills to preserve the body. He would salt the corpse thoroughly and put it out in front of his pharmacy to dry in the sun, so many residents began to follow the experiment with interest.

When Davis himself died, someone stole the mummy and sold it to a traveling exhibition. Tom was then shown as "a petrified Indian."

AMERICA'S FIRST NATIONAL FOREST RANGER

Bucking the "Git and Grab" Believers

A strapping young man of twenty years, Bill Kreutzer rode his horse into Denver from Sedalia and applied for a job as a forest ranger with the Forest Reserve system. Even though the reserves had been set aside in 1891, the laws concerning grazing, mining, and lumbering had never been enforced. In 1899 it was rumored that the federal government was going to hire forest rangers, and the first would be in the Plum Creek reserve near Bill's home. After some complications over his youth and politics, Kreutzer, the son and grandson of foresters trained in Germany, was given the appointment.

Most folks didn't want the government to restrict the use of forest lands in those days, and in his early career he was the target of gunshots more than once. Bill fought forest fires alone and was burned many times. Political pressure led to his transfer to Battlement Mesa Reserve, with headquarters at Collbran, on the Western Slope. Again there was trouble, but he broke a bronco to prove to ranchers that he was no city slicker, and they learned they could rotate grazing lands for better feed.

There were others who were not so pleased with the idea of a U.S. agent, and he was soon transferred to Cedaredge when the region was changed to Grand Mesa National Forest. He continued to promote good grazing and had to serve as a go-between in disputes between cattle and sheep ranchers. His other duties entailed trying to stop random cutting of timber, and even restricting mining operations. He was on the front line of the battle for preservation and multiple use as opposed to the "Git and Grab" philosophy of Colorado's early settlers.

Kreutzer's friendly manner, his cowboy background, and his high principles gradually won him the acceptance of ranchers, foresters, and miners and a promotion to supervisor of the Gunnison National Forest. Bill fell in love and married at Gunnison. In 1921 he was appointed supervisor of Colorado National Forest, surrounding Rocky Mountain National Park, and spent the rest of his career headquartered in Fort Collins.

When he retired in 1939, William Kreutzer had served longer than any other man in the history of the service - forty-one years.

Very few Coloradans have mountains named for them, but Mount Kreutzer, near Tincup in Gunnison County, was named for Bill, who died in 1956 at Fort Collins.

Photo of Cattleman's Day at Gunnison. Photo Courtesy P. David Smith

THE FIRST "WHITE MAN" ON THE LOS PIÑOS RIVER

Ex-Slave John Taylor Had Fifteen Wives

With a twinkle in his eye, eighty-three year old John Taylor told a reporter that he was the first white man to settle on the Los Piños River in La Plata County. His remark meant that he was the first non-Indian there.

As a black slave born in 1841 in Kentucky, Taylor ran away and joined the first Negro regiment of the Union army in 1864. When discharged two years later, he was free but did not want to become a sharecropper, one of the few options open to ex-slaves. So he re-enlisted, claiming to love army life, and became an Indian fighter. When his enlistment was up in 1870, he joined and rode with the Apaches where he married four wives. He left them to become a camp cook for a rancher.

Quickly tiring of that job, he joined a band of Utes, marrying two more wives. When he came to the Pine River, as he called it, in 1871 he settled down to a career of trapping, establishing a home there.

He left for a year to join the Navajos, marrying more wives. He then returned to the Los Piños for good, and married five more wives.

Explaining that there were at that time no laws against polygamy, he pointed out the simple marriage, in which the couple eat from the same bowl of mush. When the wife no longer wanted him, or by mutual consent, she simply put his saddle and blankets outside the hogan. That was the divorce.

When the Southern Ute Agency was established, the government paid Taylor $5,000 for his land, which became the town of Ignacio. He built another cabin, and, although he could not read or write, he became an official interpreter whenever a Ute, Navajo, Apache, Hopi or Mexican case came before the court.

John later tried to enlist in the Spanish-American war, but when the officer saw his grey hair, it was decided he was too old. When the

United States joined World War I, he would have been seventy-six years old. He dyed his hair and tried again, but when records showed he was a Civil War veteran, he was again turned down.

Because of conflicting stories and perhaps a poor memory, it is hard to say how many women he married. He had numerous children. The most conservative figure that can be given is that he had a total of at least fifteen wives before his death in 1934.

DID TOM MIX MIX TOM COLLINS?

Bartending in Lamar

Tom Mix was probably one of the most popular actors in the silent movie era and the beginning of sound movies. He also had his own circus and Wild West show which performed all over America and in England. He was saluted by one observer as the personification of "Rugged virtue in the saddle."

There is much to belie the ideal of the handsome and talented showman in regard to virtue. His private life was one of many women, much liquor, and untruthfulness. In about 1906, he and his third wife lived in Lamar. There he worked as a bartender at George Yowell's saloon. When interviewed in Denver some years later, he claimed that his role in southeastern Colorado was that of "High Sheriff of Two Buttes." Upon being told that in this country there were no such things as "High Sheriffs," he revised his role to that of Undersheriff of Prowers County. He was never a lawman in Colorado, and probably nowhere else but in the movies.

According to the director of the famous 101 Wild West show, "Tom could color a story redder than a Navajo blanket."

In his book **Wild West Shows** historian Paul Reddin noted that Mix did film several movies in the Canon City area.

It is vaguely possible that the movie star had mixed a Tom Collins in 1906, as that cocktail was invented in 1905.

THE MASTER OF HEROIC SCULPTURE

"Phimis" Also Engraved and Etched

His "Bronco Buster" and "On the War Trail" grace the Denver Civic Center. "The Pioneer Mother" still inspires Kansas City. "The Circuit Rider" is a centerpiece at Stanford University. His statue of Theodore Roosevelt stands in Portland, Oregon. Several of his sculptures may be found in the nation's capital, and others beautify cities around the world.

Alexander Phimister Proctor, or "Phimis" as they called him, was fourteen years old when his family moved to Denver. Born in Ontario, Canada, in 1869, he also had lived in Michigan where he had shown a natural talent for art. Finding the city life of pioneer Denver too confining, the family moved to Grand Lake where his father became a big game hunting guide and taught Phimis about wild animals. There the youth shot a bear and was fascinated by its powerful body. He had attended Arapahoe School in Denver but sought a career in art.

Proctor moved to New York City where he attracted the attention of artist J. Harrison Mills with a drawing of a panther. His first major sculpture, "Cowboy," was a stunning feature of the 1893 Columbian Exposition in Chicago, one of the greatest world fairs of all times. That statue won him national attention.

Proctor did not limit himself to sculpture. He made many wood engravings for books and later turned to copper etching. His greatest sculptural masterpieces were created in 1920 and 1921, after he had returned to the Colorado Rockies he loved so well.

Later, as a resident of Pendleton, Oregon, he sculpted another famous work, "The Western Sheriff," which still stands in that city. He won practically every award and honor available here and abroad for his statues, all in the heroic tradition. During his declining years, Proctor maintained homes in La Mesa, California; Seattle, Washington; and New York City. He died in Palo Alto, California, in 1950.

SAM HARTSEL WAS A FRIEND OF THE UTES

But He Was a Captive Guide

In about the middle of South Park, there is what remains of the town of Hartsel. It was named for Samuel Hartsel, one of the earliest ranchers in that region.

A native of Pennsylvania, he had come west in the Pikes Peak Gold Rush and in 1860 joined other prospectors near Fairplay. When he had no luck as a miner, he decided to establish a ranch. After the initial excitement of gold tapered off, Sam was practically alone except for the Ute Indians in the park. He became good friends with them and did some trading of much desired merchandise for the fine deerskins of the Indians.

One day he had been roaming quite a ways from his ranch when he spotted a large group of Indians. He rushed down to greet them. To his alarm, he discovered they were Cheyenne who had come over Ute Pass to raid the Utes. The invaders took him captive and led him to their leader, who told Hartsel they were lost. The Cheyenne demanded that the cowman ride next to him and show them the way, as they sought Ute encampments to attack. With no choice, Hartsel tried to lead them off from known Ute locations.

The leader did spot some Ute tracks, and that led to a camp where there were only older men and some women and children, the braves being out on a hunt. To Sam's horror, the Cheyenne killed four of the men and took prisoner several women and children.

For several days the marauders wandered around, but then they told their captive guide to show them the way out of the park. He led them to the trail, which would lead down to Colorado City.

Hartsel then expected to be killed, but the chief told him to get out of there. They let him keep his own horse. Even as he rode away, Sam expected to be shot in the back.

The murder of the Utes in cold blood left the rancher with a horrible feeling for the rest of his life.

Hartsel continued to ranch until the early years of the twentieth century. He then moved to Denver, selling his holdings. He invested his money in real estate mortgages at eight percent interest.

This pioneer of Colorado's Park County died in 1918.

Utes at Colorado Springs in 1875. Photo courtesy P. David Smith

PHOTOGRAPHY, MOVIES, RADIO, X-RAYS, AND DETECTOPHONES

• Harry Buckwalter's Many Achievements

Certainly one of the most talented and productive citizens in Colorado history was Harry Hale Buckwalter. His contributions, especially to the technological growth of the state, can hardly be overestimated.

He left his Pennsylvania home at the age of sixteen and arrived in Colorado Springs in 1884. Harry soon married Carry Fuller, and they moved to Denver. It was in that city that he became a printer, and then discovered his most exciting field, photography. Before long, he was the first newspaper photographer in Colorado, working for the *Rocky Mountain News*.

Riding in a balloon with daredevil Ivy Baldwin, Harry took the earliest aerial photography pictures in the mountain West. He invented an improved camera shutter, which he sold to a manufacturer for $100. Among his other inventions were the development of a static eliminator and some improvements in grinding tools.

Buckwalter also devised a listening mechanism that he called a detectaphone. It was a tiny instrument that could be hidden in any room and would transmit sounds by telephone...a predecessor of the "bug." It was reportedly used by the Secret Service and other law-enforcement agencies.

He became very interested in the properties of radium, and found it in the waters of several healing spas in Colorado, enhancing the allurement of those pools.

He was the first person to introduce the Roentgen Ray, now known as the x-ray, to this region. He was instrumental in the first use of x-ray photography in a court of law for a murder case in Denver.

During all this time, this remarkable man was taking still photographs, especially documenting the railroads of Colorado. His work also extended to human interest, scenery, and Indian portraits.

It was Buckwalter who showed the first motion pictures in Denver, drawing many to City Park for outdoor screenings. This led to the establishment of theaters and he became the main supply source for the movies.

When a place of entertainment needed a searchlight to draw attention, it was Buckwalter who designed and installed the spectacular devices. He built and installed one atop Pike's Peak to welcome a national Elks' convention.

He ventured into filming movies himself. Some were promotional short features to promote Colorado; these were shown to groups to attract conventions. Then he was awarded a contract as cameraman for movies, mostly Westerns, in the era before there were "talkies."

Buckwalter was given the position of Assistant City Editor of the *News*, but before long he found that the job took away too much time from his other ventures.

By the time of World War I, he and his wife had a falling out and divorced. Soon after that he met and married Katherine Paul. She was an employee of long standing with Western Union, and kept on at her career.

It was then that Harry got excited about the potential of radio. He built one of the first radio stations in Colorado, constructing the studio in his home. He and his wife both did broadcasts. When opera soprano Frieda Hempel came to Denver, they persuaded her to sing on their station, one of the earliest operatic broadcasts anywhere.

In the 1920s, Harry let Katherine become the breadwinner, and dedicated himself to becoming a househusband, developing a taste for good food he prepared.

Gradually his health declined, and he died in 1930 at the age of sixty-three.

Many of his finest photographs have been published in **Buckwalter: The Colorado Scenes of a Pioneer Photojournalist, 1890-1920**, by William C. and Elizabeth B. Jones.

COLORADO'S COLORFUL CAPTAIN CONVERSE

She Also Wrote Stories for Children

Few people have led a life as spirited as that of Mary Parker Converse. Born in Malden, Massachusetts in 1872, she was married to wealthy heir Harry Converse in 1891. The yacht Parthenia was her greatest joy, and she taught her five children the ways of seamanship. However, she separated from Harry in 1910 and dedicated herself to the writing of children's stories and songs. When World War I broke out, she joined the Red Cross and served as an entertainer for the troops. Following the war, she became interested in prison reform and was a key influence for change in Colorado's penal institutions. She made Denver her home for the rest of her life.

From 1936 until 1939, she shipped out four times to learn modern navigation techniques, even though she was already over sixty. By 1940 Mary was made a Captain in the U.S. Merchant Marine, the first woman so designated in the history of that service.

During World War II, she taught training courses in Denver for men seeking merchant marine commissions, often at her home on High Street, which was also a leading attraction for the social set. She was accepted for membership in the British Institute of Navigation, another first for a woman. This led to interviews on national radio networks, and in 1952, *Navigation* magazine dedicated an entire issue to her career.

Her book, **Kiddie Pals**, was published when she was over fifty, and at the age of sixty-seven she published a musical composition, "Sextet for Strings and Woodwinds." Then in her eighties, Captain Mary helped raise funds for the Denver Civic symphony and worked to promote the High Altitude Observatories at Boulder and Climax. She found time to write another book, **On Becoming a Mariner**, and also gave lectures. The Mary Parker Converse Seminar Room at the University of Colorado Astrophysics Building was named in her honor. Captain Mary died in 1961.

ANTICS OF THE FABULOUS "LORD" OGILVY

Practical Joker, Warrior and Journalist

Writer Forbes Parkhill called Lyulph Gilchrist Stanley Ogilvy one of the West's "most colorful and beloved characters." He was called "Lord" Ogilvy, but he never did have such a title, being the son of the eighth Earl of Arlie, in Scotland. At the age of eighteen he came with his father to inspect properties owned by the family in Colorado. He stayed on to become a rancher near the town of Kersey, east of Greeley.

He usually wore a waistcoat of the plaid of the Ogilvy clan. Lyulph was quite the social lion, both on the plains and in Denver. Being very wealthy, he frequently threw champagne parties for his friends and casual acquaintances. At one time he was on a train from Cheyenne, and when asked for his ticket he ignored the conductor. The official had the train stopped and gathered other members of the crew to throw Ogilvy off the train. Instead, the passenger threw all of the gang off and then presented them his ticket. When the locomotive reached Denver, he invited all of the crew to dinner at the Windsor Hotel.

Lord Ogilvy invited friends to his own funeral in Denver. When they arrived at the undertaker's parlor, he was indeed laid out in a coffin. After a short service, the coffin was closed and placed in a horse drawn hearse with glass windows on both sides. It seems the mortician had not informed the driver of the stunt, so when Ogilvy sat up suddenly holding a bottle for a snort, the driver leaped off the wagon and the horses stampeded as the dead man jumped to the ground. When things got in order again, the procession went on to the cemetery, where a freshly dug grave contained a keg of Scotch whiskey, and a grand wake was held.

Ogilvy enlisted in the army when the Spanish-American war broke out in 1898, and was one of the famous Torrey's Rough Riders. Then came the Boer war, and he joined the British army, riding as captain of a horse brigade. Wounded in action, he was awarded the coveted Distinguished Service Cross.

Back home in Colorado, Lyulph decided it was time to lay off the liquor, and he became a teetotaler for the rest of his life. Not as wealthy as he once was, he moved to Denver and took a job as a switchman in the Union Pacific Railroad yards.

Soon after that, the *Denver Post* made him the agricultural editor, a position he held for most of the rest of his life.

When World War I erupted, he served as a purchasing agent for the British Army. When the United States entered World War II, he tried to enlist in the army at the age of seventy-nine. Ogilvy died in Boulder in 1947 at the age of eighty-five.

NATURAL PHILOSOPHER FROM THE PLAINS
"High, Wide and Lonesome"

Though he was born in Nebraska in 1900, Hal Borland spent most of his formative years in Flagler, as related in his autobiographical **Country Editor's Boy.** As a member of the Naval Reserve in World War I, he was still too young to go to sea. He returned to help his father edit the *Flagler News* before becoming a reporter for the *Denver Post.* After that, he wandered all over the nation, reporting for newspapers and syndicated associations in New York; Brooklyn; Salt Lake City; Fresno; San Diego; Ashville, North Carolina; and Marshall, Texas. During a stint back in his beloved plains country, he edited the *Stratton Press* for a year, but then returned to national posts in Philadelphia and for *New York Times* Magazine, where he served as a regular columnist for the rest of his life.

His range of talent in writing was enormous. Although he was most famous for his works on naturalist topics, he preferred to be called a "natural philosopher," and indeed his columns were read throughout the world for the wisdom as well as the nature items. Hal Borland published three volumes of poetry, wrote radio scripts, documentary films, movies, and novels. As editor of the *Sunday Times*, Borland wrote **History of Wildlife in America.**

As novelist, he wrote for both children and adults. **Valor, the Story of a Dog** was his most popular juvenile novel, while his most honored novel was **When the Legends Die**, a story of a Ute boy from Pagosa Springs who joined the rodeo circuit. It was published in nine languages and was made into a movie. His **High, Wide and Lonesome** was another autobiography. Borland wrote some of his material under the pseudonym of "Ward West."

During his later years, Hal moved with his wife to Sharon, Connecticut, where he continued his prolific writing career, often coming back to the Colorado prairies. Hal Borland died in 1978 at Sharon.

DISARMING THE WIDOW-MAKER

Leyner's Idea Saved Many Thousands of Lives

John George Leyner was the first white child born in Boulder County, making his appearance August 20, 1860, a mile from the mouth of Left Hand Canyon. Forty-three years later, he invented the water drill for hard rock mining, saving the lives of many thousands of miners during the twentieth century.

J. George, as he was usually called, worked in Colorado mines most of his life, inhaling the dust that resulted in silicosis for so many of his cohorts. It was almost an axiom that if a man used the air-compressor drill long enough, he would get a fatal residue of rock dust in his lungs. Earlier hammer-and-drill teamwork had many dangers, but the new and speedier power drills were so lethal that they were called "widow-makers." The result was often called "miners' con" because the symptoms and deterioration were similar to those of tuberculosis, one of the dreaded diseases of that era, generally referred to as "consumption."

Leyner was an inventor as well as a miner. He experimented with several power drills and constantly faced frustration trying to design one that would produce less dust. He did come up with a drill which rotated as it drove, hammered by steam power. This sped up the process but still threw a constant backfire of dust at the drillers.

By 1903, he had discovered a whole new principle for the drill. Water was forced through a hole bored in the center of the drill bit, dampening the granules of rock and causing them to flow in a muddy mass from the drill hole. His Leyner Engineering Works, near Littleton, produced this drill for mines all over the world. While silicosis was still a danger to miners, especially with the use of dynamite for blasting, the job of a hard rock miner was no longer a guaranteed death sentence.

COLORADO'S OFFICIAL STATE LIAR

The Case of the Wooden-Legged Cat

It was 1933, and Colorado like the rest of the nation was undergoing what came to be known as the Great Depression. Banks had failed, unemployment reached a new high, and the prices of farm products and minerals had plunged.

Trying to bring a touch of levity to the situation, Governor Edwin C. Johnson decided to appoint an Official State Liar. He commented, "I have felt that too much lying was being done in the statehouse, and I ought to cut down on it. Hereafter, one man will do all our lying, and if he can't do it the way we want it done, we'll get someone else."

An informal contest was held to decide the recipient of the honor. The winner was Phil McCarty, president of a Denver heating company.

McCarty's winning story was about a cat with a wooden leg that killed mice by hitting them over the head with the leg. As the cat became cross-eyed from looking at the mice, he was no longer able to strike accurately. Nevertheless, the mice died of fright when they beheld the cross-eyed cat.

On February 1, a former president of the Ornery Men's Club of the World presented McCarty with an official rubber medal in a ceremony broadcast on a Denver radio station.

Johnson had stated that the salary for the position was to be a dollar a year. McCarty told his first official lie when he told the Governor he would not accept the payment.

THE WIVES OF CHARLIE AUTOBEES

A Vendor of Taos Lightning

It is certain that of the earliest white settlers in what became Colorado, Charles Autobees was among the most colorful. He fought Indians and married Indians. He founded a town on the Huerfano River. Settling in Colorado in 1851, Charlie knew all the other trailbreakers: Tom Tobin (who may have been his brother), "Uncle Dick" Wooton, and the Bent brothers.

He was instrumental in introducing the legendary "Taos lightning" whiskey to the traders, trappers, and miners of Colorado. Produced at Taos, New Mexico, the liquor got its name from the customers who said it made them feel as though a torchlight procession was galloping down their throats. Autobees established a distribution route over the Sangre de Cristo Mountains to the settlers along the Arkansas River, and eventually the fiery liquid made its way to several rendezvous in Wyoming.

Charlie seemed to have a wife in every Indian tribe. He married Picking Bones Woman, a Cheyenne, but later returned her to her people. He then married Serefina Avila, a Spanish lady who stayed in New Mexico when Charlie came to Colorado. Once in Colorado, he married Sycamore, an Arapahoe. When a delegation of that tribe came to take her away, Autobees and his employees fought a winning battle to keep her.

After Serefina died, Autobees married Estefana, a Navajo. He then lived with a Sioux woman for a while. When he was sixty-five years old, he married Juanita Gomez, a seventeen-year-old widow. At some time in his career he was reputed to have had a Ute wife, Maria.

When he died at the age of seventy, in 1892, he had established a wide reputation throughout the West, in addition to founding the town of Autobees Plaza in Pueblo County.

Having children by these wives has led to the estimate that he has nearly a thousand descendents now living in Colorado.

"BLOODY BRIDLES" HAD A SCHEME

Fandango Dollars

During the latter part of the 1880s, silver mining was the leading industry in Colorado. More than half of the nation's silver was produced in this state, but production was so great that the metal had lost much of its original value. As the United States abandoned silver coinage this state's economy was threatened with collapse. In 1890 Congress passed the Sherman Silver Purchase Act in order to help rescue the western mining industry.

By 1892, however, the nation was plunged into a major economic depression. There was much talk about repeal of the Sherman Act. Davis Waite, of Aspen, was elected Governor of Colorado, running on the Progressive Ticket. He also had the full support of the so-called Silver Democrats.

Waite, who was somewhat irascible in temperament, gave a speech in 1893. He excoriated the federal government, saying in regard to the prospect of repeal, "we shall meet that issue when it is forced upon us, for it is better, infinitely better, that blood should flow to the horses' bridles than that our national liberties should be destroyed." This remark made him a bit of a national celebrity known as "Bloody Bridles Waite."

Congress repealed the Sherman Act in October of that year. It meant an almost total collapse of the silver mining industry.

Waite noted that the U.S. Constitution, Article I, Section 10, forbade the states to coin money or issue paper money, but did allow each state to make gold or silver coins, either domestic or foreign, legal tender for payment of debts. The Governor's idea was to ship Colorado silver to Mexico, there to be coined into Mexican dollars, and returned for use as legal tender in Colorado. He wrote President Porfirio Diaz of that nation, "I am anxious to know upon what terms the mints of Mexico would receive and coin for us our bullion silver." When Diaz replied favorably to the suggestion, Waite called the Colorado Assembly into a special session in January of 1894.

There he proposed that Mexican dollars be made legal tender in Colorado. The legislators, on the other hand, feared that there was still a constitutional problem and in any event such a move would discredit the state. They referred to the governor's scheme as "Fandango Dollars." In spite of Waite's hope that the idea would also be adopted by other states, Colorado lawmakers turned down the proposal.

Most of the silver mines began to fill with water; the big-scale mining of silver in Colorado had come to an end.

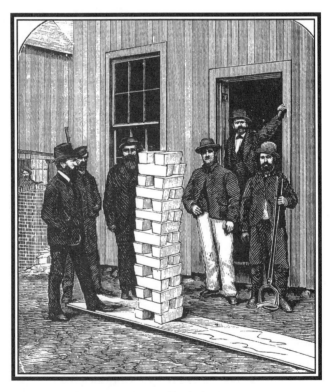

3,000 pounds of silver. Colorado: Its Gold and Silver Mines, 1879

A SAD ENCOUNTER BETWEEN FATHER AND SON
Ouray's Heartache

As a youth, Ouray, who later became the spokesman and negotiator for the Ute Indians, herded sheep for a rancher at Taos, New Mexico. At the age of eighteen, he returned to the Tabeguache Ute band in the San Luis Valley and soon after that married a maiden of that tribe. They had one son named Coatan.

When Coatan was five years old he was with his people hunting buffalo somewhere in the vicinity of the modern town of Fort Lupton, Colorado. This territory was claimed by both the Arapahoe and Sioux Indians. While the men were away from the Ute camp, the Sioux attacked and kidnapped young Coatan as a slave. By the time the men returned it was too late to pursue the attackers.

Ouray's wife fell into deep depression and died soon after this tragedy. In time, Ouray married again. This was to sixteen-year-old Chipeta. This marriage produced no children, and Ouray was desperate to find his only son.

In 1873 Felix Brunot was appointed the head of the Ute Indian Commission charged with negotiating a treaty to permit white settlement in the mining areas of the San Juan Mountains on Ute territory. This would allow miners and prospectors to develop the towns of Lake City, Ouray, Silverton, and later Telluride. He had already designated Ouray as the representative for the Utes because this leader could speak Spanish and English.

During the preliminary discussions, Ouray told Brunot of Coatan's kidnapping by the Sioux. Brunot decided he would be able to negotiate more favorably if he could locate the boy who would then be about fifteen years old. The Commissioner sent letters to all Indian agents in the region telling them to instigate a search for Coatan. The result was quite well documented: the Sioux had kept Coatan only a short time before trading him for some horses to the southern Arapahoes who were mortal enemies of the Utes. The

Arapahoes had named him Friday, and reared him as a loyal warrior on the plains of Eastern Colorado.

Satisfied that he had located Ouray's long-lost son, Brunot planned to bring the lad to a meeting at the Los Pinos Agency in August of 1873. However Coatan had not accepted the idea and had run off into the wilds to escape the U.S. military detachment assigned to retrieve him.

A little later, Brunot arranged a meeting in Washington, D.C., between the Utes and Arapahoes. This was to attempt reconciliation between the two tribes. He did get the Arapahoe delegation to include young Coatan, who did not want to go but was persuaded by his leaders to make the trip.

The father and son met in Washington, and neither could recognize the other from appearances. Ouray was convinced, though, that this was indeed Coatan. A Ute relative who had played with the boy long ago tried to get Coatan to recall their happy times, but no such memories were forthcoming.

Ouray went over family incidents that might jog the boy's memory, but still the lad insisted that he was an Arapahoe and always had been, denying any knowledge of the short stay with the Sioux.

Finally Ouray gave up and decided the youth should return to the Arapahoes as he could never be happy with a people whom he had been taught to hate. The youth could not even recall being named Coatan. Ouray was grief-stricken but never made any other attempt to claim the young man whom he believed to be his son.

Ouray, Chief of all the Utes. Photo Courtesy P. David Smith

WHEN DOUGLAS FAIRBANKS STOLE A LOCOMOTIVE

His Enrollment at School of Mines was Brief

Douglas Fairbanks, whose original name was Douglas Ulman, was born in Denver in 1883. He attended West High School there, and once, bored with study hall, jumped out of the second story window and landed on his feet, running away with the agility that was later to make him famous. Given to pranks such as greasing streetcar tracks, he was once brought before the famous juvenile judge, Ben Lindsey, and given a stern lecture.

Douglas was only sixteen years old when, somehow, he seems to have been admitted to the Colorado School of Mines. This issue has lately become a matter of dispute. He also spent a short while at Harvard before becoming a noted actor in New York and then moving to Hollywood to become one of the first, and probably the greatest, of the swashbuckling actors of the silent movies.

A very handsome man, he was the star of several flicks by 1914 when **Who's Who in America** decided to include his biography. He listed both Mines and Harvard in his resume.

Fairbanks went on with his career, at one time marrying the famous Mary Pickford, who was adored by the men as much as Douglas was by the women. When sound came to movies, he founded his own production company and continued in the limelight until his death in 1939 when the mantle of fame was passed to his son, Douglas Fairbanks, Jr.

Sixty years later, in 1999, the School of Mines was asked about Fairbanks' career there. The college archivist, Robert Sorgenfrei, made a diligent study of the records and found no enrollment information on either Fairbanks or Ulman. He further noted that the college had a policy of admitting no one under the age of seventeen. It was Sorgenfrei's suspicion that Fairbanks had included Mines in his résumé because it was such a famous school, and that it was very doubtful if the famous actor had ever attended the Colorado School of Mines.

On the other hand, if Fairbanks was such a famous movie star by 1914 as to be listed in **Who's Who**, why would he want to include academic credits?

Upon seeing Sogrenfrei's article in the alumni magazine, Robert Wheeler, class of 1941, wrote about an incidental story told by a long-respected professor, head of the Mathematics Department at Mines, during one of his classes.

Professor John C. Fitterer had a lengthy career at the college. His reputation was such that it is unlikely he was making up the story he told about Douglas Fairbanks. Further, the story is so strange that one would be hard-pressed to come up with such an event unless it actually happened.

It seems that many years ago, Mines had just won the first football game of the season, played in September against the University of Denver. The students from Golden were in a hilarious mood, and perhaps had partaken of some alcohol. Douglas Fairbanks was among them and possibly the leader, as they commandeered a railroad train which was leaving Golden on its trip to Idaho Springs. They somehow "lured the engineer out of the cab, jumped on the train and took off."

The miscreants would go up the canyon a mile or two, tooting the whistle the whole time, then back up to Golden, making much noise, then go up and return again and again until the citizens were alarmed and the law stepped in.

It is probable that Douglas Fairbanks was expelled even though he had hardly begun his first class in the school. It is also probable that he may have lied about his age in order to enroll. It is even more probable that he had not paid his tuition at the time.

At all events, it certainly fits in with the reputation the actor had all during his lifetime, as recorded by his biographers.

JUST WHO WAS "SNIKTAU"?

A Man With a Mountain of Creativity

Overlooking Loveland Pass in Clear Creek County stands Mt. Sniktau, 13,234 feet in elevation. Until 1927 it was called the Big Professor, a tribute to Engleman, a famous biologist for whom the Engleman Spruce tree was named. The story of Sniktau is one of some interest.

E.H.N. Patterson wrote for his father's newspaper, the *Oquawka Spectator*, in Oquawka, Illinois, back in the 1840s. He was probably twenty years old when he began correspondence with Edgar Allan Poe, the greatest literary figure in America at the time. Poe was not only a great poet, but has been hailed as the founder of both the short story and the mystery story.

The famous man was so impressed with the letters of Patterson that he conceived of an entirely new magazine, of the highest intellectual class, to be edited by Patterson. Poe probably did not realize the youth of his correspondent. The poet led a campaign to raise funds for this publication, to be named *The Stylus*. At the age of only forty Poe had a nervous breakdown, turned to alcohol, and died in 1849. Thus ended Patterson's potential moment of fame.

Young Patterson then joined the gold rush to California, and it was there that Indians and fellow prospectors began calling him Sniktau, which means "equal to any emergency." The young man returned to Illinois and used the nickname as his pen name. Having had no luck in California, Patterson joined the rush to the Rockies in 1858, hoping to find gold. What he found was a career as a columnist for the *Rocky Mountain News* and the *Western Mountaineer* at Golden. His columns on the developing mining industry were crisp and refreshing, all under the name of Sniktau.

He later became owner and editor of the *Georgetown Miner*, building up a reputation as one of the greatest journalists in Colorado history.

He was enchanted with the mountains. For twenty years he showed others how to appreciate the exciting landscape.

In 1927, the U.S. Geographic Board, with the blessings of the Colorado Geographic Board and the Colorado Mountain Club, changed the name of the peak to Mt. Sniktau. This was made official in 1928, a hundred years after Patterson's birth and fifty years after he was buried in the shadow of that peak.

ABOUT ARTS, MUSIC, ENTERTAINMENT, AND ATHLETICS

IS THE PEN MIGHTIER THAN THE SWORD?

Those Rural Debate Clubs

Before the days of radio, rural communities and small towns engaged in their own entertainments and forms of mental stimulation. Many towns had community bands, and then there were the debate clubs. These were not school debate teams. They were organizations of men who would challenge each other to somewhat formal debates and often meet with teams from neighboring towns. They were the pride and joy of their hometowns.

One such club, formed in a rural school district north of the town of Arriba in Lincoln County, was given to debating such topics as "Resolved: The Pen is Mightier Than the Sword." There was no choice as to sides; these were determined by drawing straws. Another topic by that club was "Resolved: It is Better to be a Homesteader in Colorado than a Tenant Farmer in Iowa." One man who was considering selling out and moving to Iowa at the time was condemned to debate the affirmative. The Hotchkiss Club held a debate with the Cedaredge Club in Delta County over the advisability of cooperatives in farm production. Many townspeople drove to Cedaredge to cheer their team on, including many who did not agree with the position required in the debate.

There were debates as to whether the United States should declare war on Germany, whether women should have the vote, and whether there should be national prohibition. Another western Colorado issue was "Resolved: The Western Slope should cecede from Colorado." In that case, the negative side won the debate.

By the 1930s, this activity seems to have died out with the arrival of sound movies and radio entertainment. Some literary societies have continued to the present, and there are still adult community bands and even symphonies, but most of the debate has been relegated to high school teams, which now include the feminine sex.

TEDDY BEARS AND CALAMATIES

Remembering Those Home Town Baseball Teams

Almost every town in Colorado big enough to gather nine willing men had its own baseball club a century ago. These were sources of community pride and enthusiasm as well as entertainment, and they played other towns with a fervor that sometimes caused long-time rivalries in business and politics.

When the coal mining town of Somerset, a few miles east of Paonia, played Telluride, a train was chartered to the latter town. It was filled with the Somerset band, team, and most of the citizens. They won over the hard rock miners.

Names of the teams were often distinctive, although there were plenty of "stockings" colors (these were later shortened to sox). There were the Pacifics, the Queen City, the Actives, the Grizzlies,

"Thrown Out On Second" by Gilbert Gaul. Harper's Weekly *September 10, 1887.*

Our Boys, and the Greeley Calamaties. Denver had several teams, including one named for Theodore Roosevelt, the Teddy Bears. Later, they dropped the Teddy and the team lasted a long time as the Denver Bears.

Most of the teams were male, but there were exceptions, as when the male Lamar Cardinals beat the Holly Bloomer Girls.

Occasionally a home town player would reach the big leagues. Joe Tinker, who played with the Teddy Bears in 1900, made the Hall of Fame later with the Chicago Cubs. He is still remembered for the famous double-play combination known as the "Tinker-to-Evers-to-Chance."[*] Another famous Denver player who made the big leagues was Charles "Babe" Adams, who won 194 games as a pitcher in the pros.

Smoky Joe Wood had his start as a youth on the Ouray team. By 1912, his fastball won thirty-four games for the Chicago Red Sox, losing only five. He won three World Series games that year, batting .290. Joe was honored by his home town for many years.

[*]*"Tinker to Evers to Chance" reads a poem by Franklin P. Adams about the Chicago Cubs' 6-4-3 double-play combination in the first decade of the twentieth century. Shortstop Joe Tinker threw to keystoner Johnny Evers who in turn threw the ball to first baseman Frank Chance. The poem was named "Baseball's Sad Lexicon."*

FIRST SKI TOW IN COLORADO

Probing the Snow for Slide Victims

Several prominent Denver men were instrumental in the creation of the first ski tow in Colorado. It was a rope tow of about a thousand feet in length, atop Berthoud Pass.

Myron Neusteter, Charles Boettcher and Jack Kendrick, all scions of Denver business families, persuaded the May Company Department Store to finance the construction of the lift.

Grand opening for the tow was on February 7, 1937. After impressive talks by several officials of the company, the five-horsepower engine started the rope in motion, and the skiers enjoyed the luxury of a ride up all during the day.

Among the skiers were two refugees who had escaped from Nazi Germany and were experienced Alpine skiers. Unfortunately, they were caught in a small avalanche late in the day. No one knew much about how to find victims of a snowslide in those days. Nearby was a camp of the Civilian Conservation Corps.

The C.C.C. was a New Deal project to employ young men on public projects during the Great Depression of the 1930s. These workers were sent for and given poles to probe for the two missing skiers. They prodded with the sharpened sticks, but never found the bodies. It was not until the snow melted in the spring that the bodies were found. One of them was mutilated with a pole hole pushed through it.

The first fatality from sport skiing other than by avalanche occurred on May 21, 1939, when Berrien Hughes ran into a rock on Loveland Pass. The Hughes Run at Winter Park was named in his memory.

The early day Berthod Pass ski lift. Photo Courtesy P. David Smith

HOW LEADVILLE LOST ITS
HOME ON THE RANGE

Did the Junk Lane Gang Forget They Remembered?

In the 1930s, Congressman Edward Taylor had printed in *The Congressional Record* that President F.D. Roosevelt's favorite song, "Home on the Range," was composed and written originally in Leadville, Colorado. Taylor had once been a school official in that city.

Indeed, in 1885, Crawford O. "Bob" Schwartz, Leader of an informal combo who lived in a Leadville cabin they called "The Junk Lane Hotel" had worked up the lyrics and music that winter. He described the details in a letter to his parents. The song had the now familiar leading words, "Oh, give me a home where the buffalo roam, and the deer and the antelope play," and pretty much the same words now familiar to millions of Americans. It was different, though, in reflecting the mining pursuits of Leadville, with:

> Oh give me a hill
> And the ring of the drill,
> In the rich silver ore in the ground.

Schwartz lived on until 1932, convinced that the Junk Lane boys were the first ones ever to compose that song. It may be that they had heard the original some time in the past and thought it a bit of folk music. Their piece was entitled "Colorado Home." It was published as the original version of the song in 1933.

That was when the controversy erupted. An Arizona couple filed suit for $500,000 for copyright infringement, claiming their "An American Home" was the first version of the song. They employed a New York lawyer to file the case.

In the investigation that followed, it turned out that neither Schwartz nor the Arizonans had a proper claim. It seems that a Kansas carpenter and musician, David Kelly, and an alcoholic physician, Browser Highly, wrote the original music and lyrics. The lyrics were published in the *Smith County Pioneer* of that state in 1873. It has since become the Kansas State Song.

It is possible that the boys in Leadville had the rudiments of the music in their minds without realizing it.

If there is a moral to this story, it will come as a surprise to very few people: don't always believe what you read in *The Congressional Record!*

Colorado home. Prospectsor's home music. Courtesy of Luther Monberg

A MOST AMAZING BILLIARDS MATCH

It Lasted Thirty-two Continuous Hours

John Quincy Adams Rollins was one of the greatest of the early developers in Colorado. He held interest in several productive gold and silver mines, was half owner of the original toll road from Denver to Central City; developed the salt works in South Park, and built the road from his namesake Rollinsville over the Continental Divide to Hot Sulphur Springs.

One summer day in 1866, when he was fifty years old, Rollins dropped in at the billiard room over Brendlinger's cigar store located at what is now Fifteenth and Blake Streets in Denver. There he met a prominent local banker by the name of Charles A. Cook. Cook considered himself a good hand at billiards, and so apparently did Rollins

They agreed to play, betting $400 per game, and to play continuously until the first man who could take no more would have to fork over a thousand dollars to the other. They marked each game on the floor with chalk.

The play started at about four in the afternoon. Rollins took several of the first games.

Crowds began to pour in and watch as evening descended and lamps were lit. Smoking numerous cigars, the contestants continued on into the early morning hours, with Cook gradually taking the lead, thinking his opponent was getting tired. Rollins then upped the ante to $800 a game.

As the sun rose, the games continued. By now, Rollins was more often on the winning side. More spectators showed up, somewhat staggered at the endurance of both men. It was going on toward midnight of that second day when Rollins decided to call off the match. It had lasted thirty-two hours.

Rollins had to forfeit a thousand dollars, but it turned out he had won $12,000 from Cook, a profit of $11,000. It seems hard to believe, but that amount of money in terms of today's economy would be in the neighborhood of a million dollars!

GENUINE FOLK MUSIC OF SOUTHERN COLORADO
The Penitente Alabados

The custom may have originated in Spain hundreds of years ago, but the practice continued in Northern New Mexico and Southern Colorado. The alabado is a song of praise that, although a hymn, is not part of any organized church. The main singers of these chants are Hispanics, especially those who have been identified as Penitentes.

Much has been written about the Brothers of Light, often called Penitentes. This is a true folk religion. When Mexico won its freedom from Spain in 1821, the Spanish priests were expelled. There were not enough Mexican priests to supply the churches of the North. It fell to the laymen to try to remember the teachings, but almost none could read, and the Biblical story was transferred to the Sangre de Cristo region.

Carried over from the earliest teaching were the ideas that only feeling the pain of Christ can suffice for misdeeds. Men alone could atone. This led to self-flagellation and other acts of pain during Holy Week. The art carvings of Christ reflected the Spanish "tragic sense of life;" saints which were never known to the Roman Catholic faith emerged. However, on Easter morning, all past sins of the family, for which the father was responsible, were redeemed. A new life could begin, free of the guilt that carries on in many more formal faiths.

Both the Church and the states forbade these practices for many years, so they were carried on in secret. Many Penitentes continued the rites in southern Colorado. Among these rites were the alabados, or sacred songs, which included such thoughts as "What Grief Can Equal that Which Lies in My Breast?", "Through the Trail of Blood," "Christ Gave Us His Body," and "Come Forth, Come Forth, Ye Sorrowing Souls."

There are still some practicing believers, although many of the traditional customs have been modified, and have been permitted by both church and state. The alabados are still sung and even recorded for posterity.

The mournful songs may depress some people, but the Penitentes and their families may also be regarded as a usually peaceful and happy lot, having expelled their troubling guilt at the time of rebirth each year. The slate has been cleaned.

THE NOTABLE STONE AGE FAIR

It all Began in a Town Called Cornish

When the Union Pacific Railroad built a branch line from Greeley to Briggsdale in Weld County in 1911, a town was created in the farming region. It was named Cornish, presumably because some of the settlers there were descendants of immigrants from Cornwall, England.

That area is rich in artifacts of the Stone Age — especially the Folsom, Plano, and Clovis cultures. It was on those plains that roaming bands of our early ancestors used primitive weapons to down animals as huge as the mastodon.

Over time, the residents of Cornish began to collect spear points, arrowheads, axe heads, and other implements which had been washed out by rain and wind. It became such a hobby that they would compare collections.

In 1934, the community decided to have a Stone Age Fair, inviting any and all to their tiny community to view the artifacts. Governor Ed Johnson arrived to dedicate the celebration which had some 25,000 items on display.

The following year, archaeologists arrived to examine the various weapons and tools. Some 10,000 people from forty-one states came to this tiny hamlet to talk about the Paleo-Indian cultures. For the next four years it continued to attract so much attention that the little town could no longer handle the crowds, so the fair was transferred to the town of Loveland, and became an annual event in that city.

As for Cornish, it dwindled in population. The church and school consolidated with those of other towns. The only store in town closed its doors. The railroad ceased its service and tore up the rails in 1966. The next year the post office was discontinued. Today there are only a few foundations, overgrown with brush and weeds where Cornish once stood.

THE GIFTED CHISELER OF STERLING

He Draws New Life from Dead Trees

There are a number of talented wood sculptors in Colorado, but perhaps the most refined products of the chisel are to be found in the city of Sterling. There are twelve spectacular works carved from dead trees while still standing.

Bradford H. Rhea came to Sterling in 1978 to work for the Nuclear Medicine Department of the Logan County Hospital. He had taken some fine arts courses at the University of Northern Colorado but found his greatest satisfaction in sculpting wood. In his spare time he began to carve on the large surfaces of logs.

Using only a chisel and a hammer, Rhea allows the form to emerge as he works. When a tree is to be removed because of disease, the city lets him know. Once the bark is stripped, the disease cannot spread. The grounds crew tops the tree, and then the artist goes to work.

In an interview he commented. "I like the freedom of removing pieces until the forms reveal themselves. All sculptures are meant to be what they turn out. I feel like a tool in the process."

Among his works, located at different spots throughout Sterling, are five "stargazing giraffes" on a single foundation, a delightful clown, and the complex "Serephim," with a lion, lamb, eagle, and representation of God all in one composition.

"Serephim" by Bradford Rhea. Photo Courtesy Author

AMERICA'S MOST FAMOUS SCOUTMASTER

Buck Burshears and the Koshare Indians

It was in 1933 that James Francis "Buck" Burshears conceived of the idea of making Boy Scout Troop 10 in La Junta into a group dedicated to the study and preservation of American Indian lore. Since then it has become the most famous troop in the nation, performing dances to which even some native tribal leaders have come to study their lost traditions. The Koshare Indians (Koshare means fun-maker) have become a model for the entire scouting program with over 500 Eagle ranks awarded during the years of Burshears' leadership.

Buck was born in Swink in 1909 and later moved to La Junta where he attended high school before enrolling at Colorado College and doing further work at St. Louis University. He was a social worker and railroad contractor, but his fame rested on his sixty-five years of volunteer work with the Boy Scouts of America.

As a college student, he became very interested in Indian lore and studied with some of the nation's leading experts on the subject. Teaching the boys the dances, Burshears gave them a basis for the unique program of performances; they made all of their own costumes and props, giving attention to absolute authenticity. He married Jane White in 1949, and she became the troop "mother" until her death in 1971.

One of the achievements of this man who received presidential citations for his work was the establishment of the Koshare Kiva in La Junta, featuring a collection of art worth millions of dollars and now a popular tourist attraction. Much of the art was donated by Burshears himself. His inspiration to thousands of scouts, both in his own troop and nationwide, was contained in his admonition, "Don't wait to become a great man; be a great boy!"

Buck continued to lead the troop until his death in 1987.

TWO GREAT BLACK MUSICIANS

George Morrison and Andy Kirk

From Boulder to a command performance before the King and Queen of England, playing a violin and leading one of the nation's great all-black orchestras, George Morrison overcame racial prejudice to take a major role in the introduction of jazz to the world. He was born in poverty in Missouri, one of fourteen children whose parents were locally noted musicians. They moved to Boulder in 1900 when George was nine years old and already playing the violin. Soon after, the family started playing the mining camps as the Morrison Brothers String Band.

Morrison married Willa May, and they moved to Denver. He had worked at odd jobs to take advanced music lessons and dreamed of playing with the Denver Symphony but racial attitudes made such a career unthinkable in those days. He did lead a band that played wherever he could; in many places he could not have attended as a customer because of his race. Beginning in parlor houses, including that of the infamous Mattie Silks, he later led an eleven-piece band at the Albany Hotel, and for many years played on the special train to Cheyenne Frontier Days.

The Morrisons had two children. The family left Denver for a time to study classical music in Chicago and discovered early jazz there. Then he formed his own jazz band and began to tour the nation. His fame led him to New York where he became a recording artist for Columbia Records. He toured Europe in 1920 playing command performances for King George and Queen Mary of England. After his return George was among the most popular bandleaders in the nation. He opened a nightclub in Denver but was forced to give up in the Ku Klux Klan revival of 1925.

However, for decades after that time, Morrison's orchestra played in Colorado and continued his national fame. One of his further contributions to music history was the introduction of Denver's Paul Whiteman to New York record studios, and the presentation of

Hattie McDaniel, another Denverite, to show business. She sang for his band on tour before her later fame as the first black person to be presented with an Academy Award.

Another person he launched into the world of entertainment was Andy Kirk. Kirk moved from either Ohio or Kentucky to Denver to live with his aunt when he was six years old in 1904. He grew up in Denver and attributed most of his success to the attentive teachers in that city.

In 1918, he was polishing shoes in Sterling and saved enough to buy a saxophone. The next year, at the age of twenty, he got his first job playing at Denver's Weir Hall for four dollars a night.

It was about that time that he joined Morrison's orchestra. Then he branched out, away from continuous jazz, to found a group called Andy Kirk and His Dark Clouds of Joy.

He later changed that name to Twelve Clouds of Joy. The band traveled by bus all over the nation performing in both large cities and smaller towns. Because of the range of such travel, the band had its headquarters in Kansas City.

Most of the fans expected straight jazz programs but were surprised that the tunes were often the sweet sounds that became popular as swing by the Thirties.

WHEN COLORADO MADE MORE MOVIES THAN HOLLYWOOD

Eaglerock Airplanes Were a Sideline

For decades, captive audiences in more than 11,000 movie theaters saw advertising shorts produced by the Alexander Film Company of Colorado.

Brothers J. Don and Don M. Alexander were the founders of the motion picture company of Englewood and later Colorado Springs. It was the largest producer of those advertising features in the world with clients including most of the manufacturers of autos, appliances, soft drinks, and chewing gum. Each of the one- or two-minute features usually had a local supplier mentioned in the ad.

Starting out in Spokane, Washington, the producers moved to Englewood, Colorado in 1923. Four years later they established a studio at Colorado Springs which grew to over twenty-six acres. By 1951, the company could proclaim that more than 10,000 theaters in the United States and another 1,400 in foreign countries were under agreement to show Alexander films.

Also in the early twenties the Alexanders had designed a new type of airplane to fly its agents around the country. The plane had a cruising speed of ninety miles per hour and was so efficient that it was in demand by other flyers. Thus was the Alexander Aircraft Company formed to produce the popular Eaglerock plane. It had the endorsement of the famous Charles Lindbergh. Only when the Great Depression set in did the company run out of buyers for the "aeroplanes." However, more people than ever were going to the movies and looking at Alexander's ads.

Gradually television became an even greater market for such promotion, and with it came far more competition. The Colorado Springs firm did produce TV commercials, but by that time the company had been sold to a New York firm. Alexander produced one of the most famous TV ads in history. It showed a 1964 Chevrolet parked atop the 2,256-foot Fisher Tower monolith in Utah.

In 1963 the firm was sold to a competitor, Motion Pictures Advertising of New Orleans.

DENVER'S FIRST ORIGINAL OPERA

It Turned out to be a Farce

Henry Houseley came to Denver from his native England in 1888 to take over as organist at St. John's Cathedral. He brought with him a great reputation, having studied with some of Europe's masters of the organ, choir, and some orchestration. Before long he had earned a reputation as director of the choir in that church. It was in 1892 that he finished composing his opera, Native Silver, the first one by a Denver citizen.

There is little doubt that the music was quite serious, but the libretto was written by Stanley Wood who had a bent for humor and satire. There were a number of jibes at Colorado politics as well as the mining industry in the lyrics.

Among the characters were Colonel Excelsior Blow who was campaigning for election to the U.S. Congress. He was supported by a "Native Silver" miners' band led by one Mendelssohn Mike who was superintendent of the Native Silver Mine. The Colonel's daughter, Pearl, was betrothed to a titled Englishman, the Earl of Kerosene. However, it turned out that Mike was actually a rich Bostonian and was madly in love with Pearl. The plot thickens as a wealthy Denver spinster, Capitola Hill, falls in love with the Earl of Kerosene, who turns out to be an impostor.

The opera was performed at the Broadway Theater April 22 and 23, 1892, and it was received with enthusiasm. This led to another performance on May 9.

That was not the only opera Houseley wrote. He followed with five others and became an institution in Denver music.

The versatile organist founded the Denver Choral Society, and from that he selected three specialized choirs to compete in the St. Louis Louisiana Purchase Exposition of 1904. Denver was the only city to bring three choirs to the contest. Of those one took third place in the competition winning a prize of $2,500.

Still later, Houseley organized one of two symphonies in Denver. He also served as Director of Music at the University of Denver.

COLORADO'S FIRST SNOWBOARDER?

A Near Disaster in the High Rockies

They were then known as Norwegian snowshoes in the early days of Colorado history, but we now call them skis. These boards were often twelve feet long and a single pole balanced the skier. They were essential for navigating the deep snows of the mountains. It was in the 1870s that a young Englishman, John Gladwyn Webb, set out one winter to seek his fortune in a search for gold. He had learned to master the skis, and he was doing well until he crossed the summit of one pass and tripped. To his horror, he had lost his vital snowshoes which had slipped loose.

Webb was able to grab one but the other slid down the slope before him leaving only a track in the powder. As the snow was at least ten feet deep, there was no possible way to wade out from his isolated spot. He would never be found, and would simply flounder and die there.

In desperation, John placed the remaining ski beneath his body and carefully balanced himself upon it in a crouched position. Guiding with his elbows, he was able to follow the trail of the missing ski to where he located it far down the slope. There he dug it out and was able to go on his way.

The slat is wider now, and it is called snowboarding and is performed in a somewhat upright posture.

REVEREND LAMB'S SLIDE DOWN LONG'S PEAK

First Recorded Descent of the Formidable East Face

It was in 1871 that Reverend Elkanah Lamb of the United Brethren Church climbed to the summit of Long's Peak above Estes Park. Without much experience, he decided to go down the steep "front" of the mountain.

The East Face of Long's Peak is one of the most challenging climbs in the Colorado Rockies, a 2,000-foot sheer cliff. A narrow ridge known as "Broadway" to mountaineers bisects it about halfway. On the south side of the surface known as the "diamond" is a sharp ravine that retains snow and ice the year round.

Lamb was able to work his way to Broadway and then followed that passage to the gap. As he started to work his way down, he lost his footing and slid hundreds of feet down the gap. As he wrote about the experience later, he had slipped and started down "faster than an arrow's rapidity."

By luck, he was able to grab hold of a solid stone overhang, and arrest the slide before he plunged even more steeply. He reached into his trousers for his pocket knife and was able to make a tiny niche into the ice by which he might be able to step to the other side and safety.

The knife had not done much before breaking in two pieces. Lamb put his left foot into the tiny cut, and with a huge lunge, threw his body to the rocks on the opposite side, and safety. From there he was able to work his way to the foot of the mountain. "I immediately fell upon my knees and thanked God for deliverance," he wrote.

It was not until 1903 that the famous naturalist Enos Mills made another descent of the main face. That formation was not climbed until 1919.

The horrifying experience did not discourage Lamb from a life in the mountains. He became the first professional mountaineering guide in the United States. His son, Carlyle, succeeded him in that career.

Today, that vertical gash is still known as "Lamb's Slide."

Long's Peak with Denver City in foreground. Leslie's Illustrated Newspaper *December 15, 1860*

DENVER'S FAMOUS PIGEON MAN

Cornish Stonecutter Jack Venning

Homing pigeon racing had a great following in the first half of the twentieth century here in America. Another popular hobby was the breeding of show pigeons, as much an art as that of dogs or horses.

A Denver stonecutter, given much to including dove designs on tombstones, was regarded internationally as a gifted practitioner of both pigeon pursuits. He had judged the Royal Pigeon Show in London's Crystal Palace as well as shows at Memphis, Toronto and in New York's Madison Square Garden.

It was said that if any showman had plucked a single off-color feather from a white bird five years before a show, Jack could spot it as he passed down the line. He could pick the probable top ten winners of races from a flock of 150, and in 1942 he picked the winner, with no previous information, of a 500-mile race before the race began.

One of the standard races was from Glendive, Montana to Denver. Participating pigeons would frequently reach speeds of sixty miles an hour as they flew over Gillette, Douglas and Cheyenne, Wyoming, to their individual lofts in Denver.

During World War I, the U.S. Army made much use of Venning's expertise in training post pigeons to carry messages on the battlefields. His home on Ninth Street was host to pigeon lovers from all over Colorado and some other states to seek his advice on both show birds and homers.

Jack often knew pigeons on sight. Once, when a homing pigeon was a bit overdue, the stonecutter spotted him atop a house in north Denver. Climbing to the roof, Venning attracted the attention of neighbors who called the police. In answer to the demands that he come down, Jack called back that he wanted to get the bird and even called out the serial band number the pigeon carried on its leg. Carefully grasping the racer in his hands, he brought it down. Venning was correct about the number.

Jack was at one time the genial head of the stonecutters' union. Many were amused by the fact that he never lost his strong Cornish accent, a legacy of his parents who had come to Colorado to mine at Central City.

When Venning died in 1944 at the age of sixty-five, Thomas Hornsby Ferril, who later became Colorado's Poet Laureate, referred to Jack as the "Evangelist of the Noble Birds."

A LONG, HARD DAY ON SKIS

Doud's Remarkable Run

Merrill H. Doud had the contract to carry the mail between Mineral Point and White Cross in the 1880s. Mineral Point was a mining town located near the top of the divide between Silverton and Lake City, at about 12,000 feet altitude.

The skis used were somewhere between eight and ten feet in length, and each probably weighed about eight pounds. The skier used a single pole to control the slats. Doud left Mineral Point before 8:00 a.m. and went to White Cross, returning that afternoon after climbing at least a thousand feet.

When he arrived back, the postman learned that a miner had just blown a portion of his hand off picking a "missed hole." A missed hole was one in which dynamite was lodged but had not gone off in the planned explosion. Medical attention was needed as soon as possible, so Doud skied down to Silverton, about 15 miles away, to get a doctor. He and the medical man returned, skiing up about a three thousand-foot rise in altitude by around six the next morning.

In all, the intrepid mailman had skied for twenty-two hours and logged fifty-two miles! With today's light skis on level ground, that would still be quite a challenge for both speed and endurance.

Early postman on snowshoes. Illustrated London Daily News 10-30-1880

A WORLD-FAMOUS AERIALIST

Ivy Baldwin's Eighty-Six Crossings of Eldorado Canyon

One of the world's most renowned aerial performers made his headquarters in Denver during the height of his career. The man just could not resist walking both tight and loose ropes across deep canyons or making parachute jumps from balloons before the era of aviation. He performed his stunts throughout the United States, Java, Mexico, Borneo, and Europe.

Willie Ivy was born in San Antonio, Texas, in 1866 and moved to Denver as a youngster. For a while, he performed with a troupe known as the Baldwin Brothers and adopted the name by which he became famous: Ivy Baldwin.

Baldwin joined the Signal Corps during the Spanish-American War and survived when his observation balloon was shot down. He contracted with Elich Gardens, a Denver amusement park, to perform regularly and made it his international headquarters.

He was the second man in the nation to make a parachute jump. (The first was his touring partner, Tom Baldwin.) His most spectacular feats, though, were probably his walks across Eldorado Canyon, 582 feet above the streambed, first on a tight rope and later on a loose rope swaying in the wind.

Dropping from high above the streets in Chicago and New York, he showed many urban dwellers their first sight of a parachute jump. Baldwin was among the first inductees to the Colorado Aviation Hall of Fame.

Late in life, he made his home at Marshdale, near Evergreen. At the age of eighty-two, he took another ropewalk across the canyon at Eldorado Springs; his eighty-sixth stroll across the ravine there! If he ever came close to falling, he never admitted it. Baldwin lived to the age of eighty-seven, dying in 1953 at Arvada.

THOSE EARLY LOW-BUDGET FLICKS

The Time the Viewers Shot Back

In the earliest days of silent movies, exciting short features were very popular. Colorado was used for filming many of them, in some cases giving Eastern audiences their first views of the Rocky Mountains. All the production really took was a good cameraman; actors and actresses could be anyone who was around.

For instance, in 1909, Edwin S. Porter came to the town of Marble to make a film to be named "The Great Bear Hunt." He brought his suitcase and camera. He had arranged for two Marble hunters to trap two bears.

The marble quarry gave its workers the day off to take part in the production. Everyone went over to the west side of McClure Pass, where the bears were being held.

The plot was simple. A lady is fishing when she spots a large bear. It is attacking so she runs away. A group of cowboys start tracking the animal and finally find it and shoot it.

A *Denver Post* reporter who came along to write up the filming was to be one of the cowboys; his wife, who came along for fun, was the actress. An Italian Count who had come to Marble to contract for marble shipments to his country was given a cowboy job, as were several of the quarry workers. One bear was released and ran free with the cowboys in pursuit. Then the other bear was released and went for some bait nearby when the cowboys shot him. It was that simple!

In another film, Denver's famous photographer, Harry Buckwalter, was filming a feature named "Robbery of the Leadville Stage." A stagecoach was rushing toward the camera and being attacked by four mounted outlaws who were shooting at the riders. A group of tourists riding their horses from the opposite direction came upon the scene and thought it was a real robbery. Two of the tourists pulled out their pistols and started shooting at the outlaws. Fortunately, they did not hit any of the actors before they found out it was all make-believe!

NATION'S WORST TEAM: DENVER BRONCOS

The Bad Old Days Before "Broncomania"

When Denver first acquired a professional football team, the Broncos, in 1961, they did not do well. The next year they won seven and lost seven. That was their best season in a decade.

During that period, the team had a total of forty-five quarterbacks. Their opponents made great fun of them. One of the members of an opposing team was reported by historian James Whiteside as saying that playing Denver was the next best thing to an open date.

Another history writer, Robert G. Athearn, quoted a writer as saying the members usually came out for the kickoff "like ladies surprised at their bath" and then purported to play football. Someone else noted that after Denver's first point-after-touchdown conversion, the team's general manager ran into the stands and wrestled with a fan for possession of the historic ball.

After the Broncos lost the ball to the Chicago Bears seven times in one game, a fan went home and wrote a suicide note: "I have been a Bronco fan since the Broncos were first organized, and I can't stand their fumbling any more." It seems that he shot himself but the head wound was not fatal and he may have lived to see his team win Super Bowls.

WHERE THE PRO BASEBALL SCOUTS SHOW UP EVERY YEAR

More Than Four Decades of the JUCO World Series

Every spring, players in 347 two-year college baseball teams throughout the nation have a dream of reaching Grand Junction. Since 1959, that city has been host to the national championships known as the JUCO World Series.

During the last week in May, pro baseball and four-year college scouts show up to see some of the best players in the nation. Playoffs in ten regions of the United States determine which teams will show up each year to vie for the championship.

Grand Junction was chosen when it still had a junior college but has developed such a support base and facilities that it has been the host city ever since. Despite the lack of a local contender, as many as 122,000 fans have been on hand during the nineteen games of the series. One game alone attracted 10,311 viewers. These National Junior College Athletic Association playoffs perform on Grand Junction's splendid Suplizio Field.

Local service clubs and lodges adopt different teams serving as individual hosts. They take the players on tours of the Grand Mesa and Colorado National Monument.

As only one example of success, Kirby Pucket played for Triton Junior College of Illinois and went on to fame in the Minnesota Twins. A few of the other JUCO players who landed pro careers include Jay Buhner, Jim Leritz, Donnie Moore, Mike Devereaux, Kevin Ritz, Otis Nixon, Curt Shilling, and Mark Grudzeilanek.

On the eve of each series, a banquet is held. Guest speakers at this event have included Lefty Gomez, Whitey Ford, Ernie Banks, Bowie Kuhn, Reggie Jackson, Tommy Lasorda, Bob Gibson, George Steinbrenner, Stan Musial, Marv Throneberry, Paul Malitor, and George Brett.

WHEN PADEREWSKI AND CORBETT PREMIERED IN DENVER

Music vs. Athletics

Ignace Jan Paderewski first came to Denver in April of 1893. He was already considered by many to be the finest pianist in the world. Tickets were so much in demand for his concerts at the Broadway Theater that scalpers who purchased them for three dollars were able to sell them for six dollars. Paderewski was guaranteed $2,500. The concerts were scheduled for Monday and Tuesday, April 17 and 18. The Polish community in Denver was wild with enthusiasm as this was the greatest of their countrymen ever to appear in Denver.

That same week, "Gentleman Jim" Corbett, world heavyweight boxing champion, was to have his first matches in Denver. Corbett had won the title by knocking out John L. Sullivan in the twenty-first round on September 7, 1892. Boxing fans were very excited over seeing two championship events slated for Wednesday and Thursday, April 19 and 20th. It was reported that Corbett was guaranteed $40,000 for the appearances! The local newspapers made much of the disparity between the two in regard to the dollars involved, judging that quality is to be determined by money involved.

The concerts were up to the great expectations of the pianist, evoking standing ovations.

Some of the concert-goers went to the boxing matches later that week. Of course Corbett won easily, retaining his title and thrilling Denver sports fans. As a matter of fact, it was not until 1897 that he lost to Robert Fitzsimmons. He then tried a comeback with two fights against Jim Jeffries but retired after his 1903 loss to that famous pugilist.

Paderewski continued in his career and was a leader in gaining support for Poland in World War I. Following the war, he served as Prime Minister of that nation for a short time before returning to the keyboard. He continued to perform all over the world almost to the time of his death in 1941.

WHY ARE WE CELEBRATING?

From Ticks to Tumbleweeds

Many towns in Colorado have their special festivals to celebrate agricultural products or mining or other centers of interest. Some are a bit unusual.

Heeney, on the shore of Green Mountain Reservoir in northern Summit County, has an annual Tick Festival. At Springfield, the observance of the vernal equinox became so popular that they added another festival to celebrate the autumnal equinox.

At Cheyenne Wells in July, there is the Tumbleweed Festival, during which, in addition to other events, baseball teams come from far and near to play around the clock continuously for the whole weekend.

Fruita has a May observance known as Mike the Headless Chicken Day. It is in memory of a rooster who survived a beheading in 1946. It seems a bit of the brain stem was still intact, and the chicken lived for eighteen more months, being fed with an eye dropper. He even made a couple pages in *Life* magazine.

There must be hundreds of corn festivals in the nation, but it is doubtful that any other town as small as Olathe, with fewer than 2,000 people, could match the popularity of the annual "Olathe Sweet" Sweet Corn Festival. In 1999 it had grown in popularity until it attracted more than 25,000 people who consumed some 75,000 ears of the famous corn.

Sculpture by Lyle Nichols. Mike the headless rooster. Photo by author

STRENUOUS FOOT RACES

For the Challenge, Not the Glory

Thousands of Coloradans and men and women from other states and nations take part in many distance and high-altitude foot races every year. These have no corporate sponsors, very little promotional hype, and even less in the way of a prize. Participants run up mountains, over high passes, down into canyons and across stretches of plains.

As only one example, there is the Leadville 100 mile race held in August each year. Racers must complete this run within thirty hours, if they can last that long. The course takes them around two lakes, over the shoulders of the two highest mountains in the state, over 12,600 foot Hope Pass to the ghost town of Winfield, above timberline. Then they must return by the same route.

Begun in 1983, the race attracts about as many women as men. It is interesting that the largest number of racers are between thirty and fifty years of age. Record time for the race has been seventeen hours and five minutes. In 2000, there werre 407 starters at 4:00 a.m. on a rainy Saturday morning. By Sunday at 10:00 a.m. only 175 had completed the run.

Many competitors in these races condition themselves the year around. Their reward is the satisfaction of having taken part; no matter if one doesn't complete the course, the victory is not always in the consumation but in the quest!

ABOUT
INTERESTING
PLACES

THE DISCOVERY ON MULDOON HILL

Even Greater than the Cardiff Giant!

On the south side of State Highway 78, about thirteen miles southwest of Pueblo and seven miles northeast of the town of Beulah, a knoll called Muldoon Hill can be seen. This was the site where a shepherd's son started to dig a cave in 1878 when he came upon a huge petrified man, the Solid Muldoon.

Almost two decades earlier, the world had been taken in by a hoax known as the Cardiff Giant, the ten-foot tall prehistoric remains of a man found in Wales. People were thrilled at the discovery recalling Genesis 6:4, "There were giants in the earth in those days." It turned out that this was a manufactured stone carving, the plot of one George Hull, of Birmingham, New York. Hull had made thousands of dollars exhibiting the stone man before admitting that he had invented the artifact. After people laughed at themselves over this fake, they soon forgot about it. Thus it was that Hull once again created an even larger and more exacting statue, using a mallet with pins in the head to show the pores of the skin. Somehow he arranged for a geologist named Conant to be a part of the trick, and Conant probably arranged for the boy to find the giant.

Perhaps Colorado was too far from the East to have heard much about the earlier hoax. At any rate, the new find was met with great enthusiasm. After it had been exhibited at fifty cents per person admission in Pueblo and Colorado Springs, a $2,000 interest in it was purchased by the famed promoter of the sensational P.T. Barnum who was aware that it was a fake but could be shown in the circus for more profits.

In due time, Hull once again claimed the hoax, wishing to get a second laugh at the American public. In spite of that, the name Solid Muldoon captivated the imagination of several promoters. One was a prizefighter who adopted that name. The other was David Day, the colorful journalist who named his newspaper in Ouray, and later Durango, after the "giant of the earth."

AN EXCITING SUNDAY SCHOOL HIKE

Discovery of the Cave of the Winds

It was a beautiful day for a hike. The Rev. Mr. R.T. Cross's Sunday School class from the Colorado Springs Congregational Church had been anxiously awaiting Saturday, June 26, 1880, when they would go for an outing near Manitou Springs.

It was a group who called themselves the "Boys' Explorers Association." They were having a nice climb when two of the younger members strayed away from the well-defined path. Other members of the group began looking for the missing explorers. Soon the two lads were found at the entrance to a cave.

The group had brought candles with them in anticipation of a campfire gathering in the evening following the climb. They looked into the cave and lit their candles to discover the hole was ten feet long and four feet wide. Crawling through a crevice, they were amazed to find grottos with stalactites hanging like curtains, rank after rank. Beneath them were rudimentary stalagmites growing from the floor. The room was about sixty feet high and forty feet long. That led to another cavern, even more spectacular. What they had discovered became one of the region's most popular tourist attractions, the Cave of the Winds.

As often happens, other individuals later announced that they had known the caverns were there all the time. In any event, it was this discovery that led to the systematic exploration of the magnificent formations and to the attraction, which still lures thousands of visitors every year.

Early postcard scene of Cave of the Winds. Courtesy of P. David Smith

THAT STUNNING "CHRIST OF THE ROCKIES" STATUE

A Momentary Blessing for Motorists

People driving along U.S. 285 between Denver and Fairplay are sometimes amazed to look up and see a huge statue of Christ overlooking the Catholic Camp Santa Maria del Monte. It is located about two and a half miles east of the town of Grant.

At the time it was placed there in 1934, it was the largest religious statue in North America. A gift of Mr. and Mrs. John L. Dower, it stands 1,500 feet above the South Platte River Canyon.

The statue itself is thirty-seven feet tall and is mounted on a base designed by the famous Denver architect, Temple Buell. The pedestal is twenty-two feet high, thus giving the structure the size of a five-story building. It was built of terra cotta by the Denver Terra Cotta Company and was inspired by a smaller statue on the J.K. Mullen plot in Denver's Mount Olivet Cemetery. Wes Teeple drew the sketches and supervised the construction.

Christ of the Rockies Statue. Photo by Randy Fay

THE LEGENDARY CHALK CLIFF TREASURE
Death to Those Who Would Seek It!

It seems that the most inaccessible places in Colorado are those about which hidden treasure stories are told. One site that continues to intrigue the curious is the formation known as the Chalk Cliffs at the southern edge of Mount Princeton, near Buena Vista. This geologic oddity towers over Chalk Creek between the village of Nathrop and the ghost town of Saint Elmo. It is composed of kaolin clay, the result of the weathering away of feldspar material. It is more than somewhat inadvisable to go climbing on those cliffs. They tend to collapse suddenly from the weight of a human clinging to the crumbly surface.

At Mount Princeton Hot Springs, below the cliffs, there was once the magnificent Antero Hotel. Vacationers would enjoy dips in the warm water pool which has survived to the present day. They would also hear the story of the treasure in the Chalk Cliffs.

When the region was still a part of Spanish territory, covetous gold seekers raided an Indian pueblo in present New Mexico and looted the gold and silver trinkets. Followed by the angry Indians, they sped up through the San Luis Valley and into the upper Arkansas River area overlooked by what is now named Mount Princeton. Realizing it was the heavy burden they were carrying that threatened their progress, they decided to hide the loot. Placing the treasure in two mule skins, they dropped it from above into the chalk cliff formation.

It seems that the Spanish thieves were caught and all but one were killed. The survivor was wounded but eventually made his way back to civilization where he told the location of the treasure but died before he was able to return to the Chalk Cliffs.

According to legend, at least two men have fallen to their deaths in trying to find the treasure. One of those was as late as the 1880s. If there is any gold and silver in the formation, it was probably covered centuries before from the natural erosion of the cliffs which tower hundreds of feet.

UNDERGROUND BREAD-MAKING IN ARVADA

A Hot Time in the Old Town

Now a city of some hundred thousand population, Arvada has done much to hold on to the atmosphere of the days when it was a small town isolated by farms from the metropolis of Denver. Included in this effort has been preservation of the Arvada Flour Mills built in 1925.

The following Spring, the firm had its official opening. A contest was held to give a distinctive name to the flour, and the winning entry, "Arva-Pride," netted a $25 prize.

Years later, Cora Beghtol recalled a hot summer day when she had just arrived in Arvada from Kentucky. She decided to bake some bread from the local flour. What she did not know was the effect of the mile-high altitude on baking. She used her recipe from her back-home state. When she mixed it all together, it simply wouldn't rise.

As Mrs. Beghtol didn't want to tell anybody about the failure, she took the mix into the backyard and buried it. As she wearied in the afternoon heat, she went outside to sit for a while in the shade of a tree. Before long, she saw the ground begin to rise. It was the bread coming through the dirt.

It is a bit hard to believe, but that may have happened.

The Arvada Flour Mill today. Photo by Nancy Lewis-Lenyz

HASWELL'S LITTLE CALABOOSE

Smallest Jail in the Nation

Without dispute so far, the town of Haswell has the smallest jail in the United States.

Located on Colorado Highway 96 in Kiowa County, the town has fewer than a hundred residents today, although it may have had six times that many in the days before the "Dust Bowl" of the 1930s. It was one of the stops on the Missouri Pacific Railroad which named towns in alphabetical order west of the Kansas border. The popular belief about the name is that it was a town that "has a well."

In 1921 the jail, measuring only ten feet by ten feet, was constructed of reinforced concrete and contained a cell of reconstructed steel. It was used to keep drunks overnight and on at least two occasions housed thieves who were soon sent to the county jail at Eads. There are conflicting reports as to whether anyone ever escaped the jail. Some swear there were never any breakouts; others claim that an inmate could pick the lock from the inside.

Occasionally some of the men of the town would use the jail for a poker party, supposedly unbeknownst to their wives. The town Marshall admitted he was tempted to lock them in as a joke. After some ten or fifteen years the key to the bastille was lost, and the jail hasn't been used since.

Either the key has been found or the door broken in because today it has been cleaned and furnished with a mannequin which may be viewed through the barred windows. The neatly whitewashed landmark adjoins what is now the town park.

HOME ECONOMICS COURSES
INSPIRED AT GEORGETOWN

"Good Food Leads to Well-Being"

One of the main attractions in the town of Georgetown is still the Hotel De Paris built in 1875 by Louis Dupuy. Dupuy had come to that town as a miner, but after an injury he turned to the hotel profession and his special art of fine cookery.

In a short time his establishment was regarded as one of the finest places to enjoy a luxurious meal anywhere in the mountain West. Blue point oysters were brought in from Long Island, New York; caviar from Russia was available. Even game animals of Colorado were served in savory French style considered a mystery to other chefs in this state.

It was to Dupuy's dining room that a leader in American education came during the 1880s. Dr. James E. Russell was at that time the dean of Teachers' College, Columbia University, and was touring the West.

Teachers' College, Columbia, has been the single most important institution in history for directing the path of public education in America. When it endorsed an idea, the schools of the nation usually followed revising their curricula to fit the new pattern. Even at that time the college was advocating more practical and useful courses for high school students who had previously studied only college prep topics, no matter what their status in life or prospects for employment. Columbia would eventually introduce the ideals of its philosopher John Dewey as "progressive education."

A first hint of this revision occurred at the Hotel De Paris. Russell was very impressed with the fine food there and befriended Dupuy, who was considered the philosopher of Georgetown as well as a great chef.

Dupuy mentioned that there was more to food than mere survival. "Good food leads to well-being," he was reported to have commented on several occasions. Russell stayed around and learned from the master the little nuances that made his meals into gourmet treats. It was then that the dean decided that there should be courses in "domestic science" offered in the nation's secondary schools. These usually came to be known as "home economics."

By the time of Dupuy's death in 1900, hundreds of school systems throughout the nation were offering home economics as part of the curriculum.

Georgetown from Fossett's, Colorado: Its Gold and Silver Mines, *1876*

WHEN THE TOTAL ECLIPSE HIT BRANDON

Chickens Went to Roost

There were only five total eclipses of the sun which passed over the United States in the twentieth century. One was visible for only a second. Two others occurred in areas of doubtful weather conditions in the northeast and northwest. The first, though, swept from Oregon to Florida on June 8, 1918. It was a day of much excitement at the village of Brandon in Kiowa County, Colorado.

Early in May astronomers, under the direction of John Miller of Swarthmore College and E.C. Sipher of the Lowell Observatory, arrived in Brandon to make preparations. The town was selected because it was one of only two spots where the eclipse would be total; the two were within a few miles of each other. The arid climate bode well for a clear sky on the scheduled day.

Brandon's brick schoolhouse was selected as the laboratory. A tower fifty feet high was constructed of wood to support the housing for a sixty-foot-long telescope, jutting out from the building, aimed at the exact position of the sun at 5:35 p.m., when the sun would be completely blocked out by the moon. Sheds were constructed to house smaller telescopes. The scientists treated the citizens around Brandon to a series of lectures on the phenomenon.

At last the great day arrived and it dawned clear as had been hoped. If a rain or dust storm had come in, the efforts would all have been in vain.

Skies began to darken about 4:30 that afternoon. Cowboy Billy Dawson was riding his horse into town and noticed that by 5:00 the chickens were going to roost thinking it was the end of the day. Wildflowers began to close their petals.

Exactly on the predicted schedule cameras caught the perfect eclipse of the sun and the cameras took historic pictures of the corona. It first showed tiny points of brilliant light, known as Bailey's beads, slipping through the valleys on the surface of the moon and proving its surface was not smooth.

For only 88.2 seconds the sun was hidden, moments after the same thing had happened on Milton Thompson's ranch a few miles away. Total time for the partial eclipse was about two hours.

Those photographs were the best ever taken of a solar eclipse before the invention of the chronograph, a telescope which could block out the sun at any time. The first one was placed at Climax, Colorado, on the Continental Divide in 1952. It was built and maintained through the joint efforts of Harvard University and University of Colorado.

That invention made such elaborate preparations for an eclipse unnecessary. Brandon's moment of worldwide fame would not occur again, at least as an astronomical center.

FRIVOLITY IN THE GRAVEYARD

Postscript to a Noted Epitaph

The words on the stone markers have appeared several places in Colorado cemeteries and presumably in other parts of America.

The inscription is in a graveyard at the old mining town of Caribou and was reportedly at the ghost town of Vicksburg but has since disappeared possibly into some tourist's recreation room. There are probably other ones in the state.

The most frequently seen is that atop Kebler Pass west of Crested Butte. It is the only remaining marker in the Ruby-Irwin cemetery,and stands beside the road.

Mary Bronbraugh was the first person buried from the nearby camp of Irwin. She died in 1881 at the age of seventeen from diphtheria just four days before she was to be married. The inscription reads:

> "My good people as you pass by,
> As you are now, so once was I.
> As I am now, soon you must be,
> Prepare yourselves to follow me."

At one time, someone had attached a plaque to the stone, reading:

> "To follow you I'm not content,
> Until I know which way you went."

An early gravestone. Photo by Ken Rehyer

THAT MAGNIFICENT MINERAL PALACE
Home of Old King Coal and Queen Silver

They gave William H. Harvey the nickname of "Coin" because he was such an outspoken advocate of free coinage of silver in the early 1890s. After the Sherman Silver Purchase Act was repealed, a blow to Colorado's mining economy, Harvey became the campaign manager of U.S. Presidential nominee William Jennings Bryan in 1896 and may have been the real author of the famous speech in which Bryan pled with the nation, "Do not crucify us on a Cross of Gold."

A native of West Virginia, Coin Harvey was born in 1851. He became a teacher and lawyer before coming west to develop real estate.

It was all Coin Harvey's idea when Pueblo raised $150,000 to construct an impressive Colorado Mineral Palace in 1890. It became one of the "must see" attractions for tourists to Colorado during the forty-six years of its splendid existence. Alas, more attention went into the decorations than to the building itself which was constructed of wood disguised to look like stone. By 1936 it had deteriorated so much that the New Deal WPA workers had to demolish it.

Almost a city block in size, the edifice, designed by architect Otto Bulow of Pueblo, was capped by a dome seventy-two feet high and twenty smaller domes. Elaborate stone columns graced the facade. Inside there was a huge stage flanked by two large statues. Old King Coal seated on his throne was carved of coal from the Trinidad area. It was fourteen feet in height. The town of Aspen furnished a silver-plated Queen to sit opposite the King.

Ten thousand people could fill the space in front of the stage, according to estimates. Surrounding this arena, two miles of glass cases enclosed the finest specimens of almost every mineral representing almost every mining area of Colorado.

Surrounding the palace itself was a park with a boating lake, bandstand, zoo, and botanical garden. Part of the park was salvaged after a highway took some of the grounds.

As for Coin Harvey, he went to Missouri and embarked on a resort development planning a tall obelisk which would have the history of this civilization embedded in the base. There would be some sort of code for extraterrestrials to translate the text and learn what a wonderful culture this was before its demise.

His own demise occurred in 1936 with the tower still not finished, and his Crystal Palace destroyed.

The Mineral Palace. From Colorado's Enterprising Cities, *1893*

WHEN THE CAMELS CAME TO BENT COUNTY

Acabajal and his Roving Dromedaries

In the 1840s, two visionary men were instrumental in experiments by which camels from Turkey, Egypt, and Tunis were brought to the United States to traverse the desert lands from Texas to California. The idea was that of Henry Wayne, an army officer who proposed the plan to use the desert animals. Brigadier General of California, Edward Beale, pushed the idea in Congress, and eventually at least seventy-eight head of the dromedaries were brought to Texas for training as army pack animals.

Beale did prove that they could be used with successful drives across the Southwest in the late fifties. Unfortunately, though it was no failure on the part of either the trainers or the camels, the Civil War intervened and the great experiment had to be abandoned. Beale apparently bought most of them and took them to his California ranch. Some of them either were sold or strayed and wandered into Colorado.

They were accompanied by one of the herders who had been brought over from Smyrna (now Izmer), Turkey. His name was Jacob Acabajal. It was probable that he was the man who stayed near the herd of about eighteen camels as they grazed the land forty miles south of Las Animas.

Many years passed, and the accounts of camel sightings were regarded as mere legend. Henry Reyher of the town of Wiley in Bent County was not so sure. He interviewed pioneers who had seen the animals, and finally established that there really had been camels roaming the plains in the earliest days of settlement. Reyher even found out that Jacob Acabajal had died in the county in November of 1902. Whether the herder had stayed with the animals or simply left and entered another occupation was never determined.

Unfortunately, the camel experiment was never resumed after the war. A decade later the iron horse would begin to bring more modern transportation across the vast expanses of deserts.

THE RISE AND FALL OF CUSTER CITY

A Pre-Fab City in 1902

Rome may not have been built in a day but Custer City, up from Silver Cliff, was! It was located between the towns of Querida and Rosita in Custer County. Two New England millionaires wanted to show the world a model town based on mining.

On June 11, 1902, a great celebration was held on the site. George A. Custer's marble statue was unveiled as his widow looked on in pride. Governor James B. Orman and Lt. Governor Alva Adams both gave speeches. This ceremony was followed by various festivities and free beer. There were a baseball game, a drilling contest, and racing.

That afternoon the town went up. It had already been supplied with a water system into every lot. Pre-fabricated buildings were brought in from their nearby locations on wagons which had been kept out of sight until the amazing event. Probably thirty houses were put together in a matter of hours, in addition to a church, bank, saloon, school, and railroad station. There was a newspaper office, and by evening of that exciting day the *Custer City Guidon* newspaper was on the streets.

A few families of miners did move into the houses. A sewer line, fire hydrants, and electrical connections were installed. So far as can be determined the church had no minister or services, and the bank never opened. The saloon did some business but competition from towns nearer the mines was a problem. Worst of all, the arrival of the railroad which was supposed to make shipping of ore much less costly never took place. Whatever negotiations had been made for that service seemed to have broken down.

Within less than a year, many of the pre-fabricated buildings had been sold for ridiculously low prices and moved to Rosita and Querida. Soon there was nothing to be seen at Custer City except for fireplugs and the concrete foundations on which the structures had been set. No one seemed to know what became of Custer's statue.

A PILGRIMAGE TO AN OLD, LONELY CHURCH

Honoring Saint Isidore at Saint Joseph's

Autobees Plaza, one of the earliest settlements in what is now Colorado, was established on the east bank of the Huerfano River three miles above its confluence with the Arkansas River. Charles Autobees, a noted trapper and later a distiller of whiskey, founded the community in 1853.

While the original town has been washed away in various floods, there still remains the old Saint Joseph's Catholic Church. It is not far from the modern town of Avondale. Historian Ralph Taylor estimated that Autobees, who had several wives (some at the same time), may have had as many as 700 descendents by the mid-nineteenth century, with many of them still living in that region of Pueblo County.

In 1899 two of his sons, Tom and José, built the church building which is now used only two times a year. One of the most popular saints among farmers is Isidore who died on May 15, 1170. Born in Madrid, Spain, Isidore became a farmer and was believed to have been aided by angels who enabled him to plant more quickly and grow better crops than anyone else.

A folk version of the story has him in the Penitente region of New Mexico and Colorado. There he was ploughing on a Sunday morning and was told by an angel he must attend mass. When he returned, the field was ready for planting. One of the favorite Santos carvings for that region shows him with the angel on his plough.

In any event, his death has been remembered on May 15 for over 800 years in Spain and the New World. In Saint Joseph's Church there is a statue of this honored man who was canonized in 1622.

Every year pilgrims come to the isolated chapel to form a procession carrying the statue to an adobe structure known as Buena Vista (good view) about 700 feet away. There a feast lasting some twenty-four hours is held. Seeds that have been blessed are planted on farmlands which have also had a blessing in hopes of a good harvest.

THE FAIRY CAVES OF GLENWOOD SPRINGS

A Chain of Chambers Two Miles Long

They had been closed to the public for eighty-two years. In 1999 the so-called "Fairy Caves" at Glenwood Springs were re-opened for tourists under the name of the Glenwood Caverns. These underground chasms are among the geological wonders of Colorado.

It was in 1886 that Charles Darrow, homesteader of the land high on Iron Mountain, first opened them. It was believed the caves were about a thousand feet in length. The fanciful formations of stalactites and stalagmites inspired the name of Fairy Caves. When the famous Colorado Hotel opened in 1893, one of the attractions was a donkey ride to the subterranean world which was lit by electric lights.

Various problems led to the closure of the caves in 1917. In 1960, some spelunkers discovered a small hole they called a "jam crack" at the rear of the last chamber. Crawling through that aperture, they found a huge network of additional chambers, extending almost two miles.

In 1999 Steve Beckley, an engineer and cave enthusiast, leased the land and opened the attraction to the public once more.

A formation at the Fairy Caves. Courtesy of Glenwood Caves

A CONTROVERSIAL CABIN ON BOULDER CREEK

Left Hand and Bear Head Disagreed

John R. Rothrock was one of the earliest permanent settlers in Boulder County. He came to Colorado with a caravan of prospectors led by Captain Thomas Aikins in 1858. When they reached Fort Saint Vrain at the confluence of the Saint Vrain and South Platte rivers, Aikins and Rothrock decided to do some exploring on their own. On the seventeenth of August that year they pitched their tents at a place called Red Rocks on Boulder Creek.

Nearby, the southern Arapahoe Indians, led by Chief Left Hand (his Arapahoe name was Niwot) were encamped. When the white men feared the winter would be too severe, they decided to build a cabin on the site. Left Hand came to them and told them to leave as they would cut the timber which would cause the game to go away. They gave Left Hand some gifts and gave him "some good meals" and told him that he was their "great advisor." So Left Hand agreed that they could stay. However, another chief, Bear Head, was disgusted with Left Hand for being so easily persuaded so he came and told the men to get out in three days or their cabin would be burned and they would be killed. Rothrock and Aikins fortified their structure and prepared for the worst.

On the third day, Bear Head returned holding a white flag. The Indian told them that he had dreamed that Boulder Creek flooded and washed all the Indians away but the white men's cabin had withstood the deluge. Bear Head took that as a sign that the great spirit did not want the white men disturbed. They could stay!

Aikins left soon after but Rothrock remained and settled on land which became one of the first irrigated farms in the county. He married Eliza Buford in 1867, moved to Longmont and joined with Sam Williams to form a dry goods business.

THAT OLD BURLINGTON MERRY-GO-ROUND

The Kit Carson County Carousel

There is a very special building at the fairgrounds of Kit Carson County in Burlington. It houses a National Historic Landmark: the only carousel in the U.S.A. with hand-carved animals which still has the original paint.

The merry-go-round was built in 1905 by the Philadelphia Toboggan Company and features forty-six animals. They do not rise and fall as in later carousels but may be ridden to the music of the original Wurlitzer Military Band Organ.

First owner of the ride was Elitch Gardens in Denver. In 1928 the Kit Carson County Commissioners bought it from that amusement park for $1,250.

The carousel has been carefully watched over and maintained by the county ever since the acquisition. It operates for the public daily during the afternoon and evening between Memorial Day and Labor Day each year.

Animals on the Burlington Merry-Go-Round. Courtesy of Kit Carson Carousell Assocciation

AN EXCELLENT MEAL SERVED IN A CAVE

A Stage Station on the Smoky Hill Trail

The original site of Cheyenne Wells was about five miles north of the present town of that name. There was located a cave previously occupied by Indians from which flowed the wells which made an oasis in the arid plains lands. It became a stage stop on the route of the Butterfield Overland Dispatch, and later Wells Fargo.

In 1866 a reporter for the *Chicago Tribune*, Bayard Taylor, made the journey out to Colorado to report on the conditions in the frontier state. He noted that people were living in the cave, and they served him dinner there.

After describing the cavern as a natural cave extending thirty feet into a knoll of conglomerate limestone, he wrote that he was served dinner within the grotto. It was an "excellent meal" of antelope steak, tomatoes, bread, pickles, and potatoes. He added that it was a delight "after two days of detestable fare."

When the Kansas Pacific Railroad laid its tracks to the south, it ended the era of stagecoach travel on the old trail. Their line became the site of the modern Cheyenne Wells. The cavern still supplied a service as a shelter for horses and cattle during storms, and many people came to get water from the springs. Rattlesnakes also liked the place and became so numerous that ranchers finally had to use dynamite blasts to rid the cave of its pesky invaders.

Antelope being shot from a train. Harpers Weekly *May 29, 1875*

THAT POPULAR WILDWOOD LODGE
NEAR OLD DILLON

Where Motorists, Buses, and Truckers Pulled In

"Open twenty-four hours a day, seven days a week, twelve months a year. Three hundred and sixty-five days out of each year. One thousand, four hundred and forty minutes of each day. In other words, we are open thirty-one million, five hundred, thirty-six thousand seconds each year." So read the sign in the dining room of Wildwood Lodge, a place almost every motor traveler on the route from Denver to Grand Junction, Breckenridge, or Leadville knew, and where most of them stopped to catch their breath.

It was a bus stop where one changed going from Leadville to Denver. It was the foremost stopping place at the west end of Loveland Pass in the days before the Eisenhower Tunnel was built east of Vail Pass and north of both Hoosier and Fremont Passes.

During the 1950s truckers would stop for coffee and inquire of other drivers whether they had seen such and such a truck stopped in the snowstorm on Loveland Pass, or to inquire as to winter conditions ahead. It was filled with signs, some marginally off-color, but not enough to offend families who stopped there.

A man named Art James who was rumored to have made his money selling moonshine whiskey built it in 1938. He made the original furnishings for the bar and the ten sleeping rooms upstairs which could be rented to weary travelers for the night or day.

After World War II Harold Minowitz bought the property and made it into the busiest restaurant in those parts of the mountains. There was always someone there to serve whatever meal was wanted any time of day or night: breakfast, lunch, or dinner.

When the Dillon Dam was built, that ended the career of the lodge. The site was inundated by the Dillon Reservoir. The building still exists as the Elks Lodge in Silverthorne where it was moved in two sections and reassembled.

THAT MYSTERIOUS TOWER ON HIGHWAY 59

A Monument Built by the People

It is thirty-four feet high, built of 110 tons of flint, and topped by a wagon wheel. It stands beside State Highway 59 between the towns of Kit Carson and Seibert, exactly on the midpoint between the north and south borders of Colorado. Signs along the highway note that it is a "point of interest" but if one stops to find out what this structure is about, he or she will be disappointed. There is not one word of explanation about the fervent effort of a hundred inspired residents of the Great Plains.

This tower was dedicated in 1954 with state officials and historians taking part in the ceremonies which culminated a massive effort to salute the old trails which crossed that region. Known as the Old Trails Monument, it stands approximately on the Smoky Hill Trail which brought the first gold seekers to Denver. Citizens of the town of Kit Carson and nearby ranches had long dreamed of this memorial and worked for years to see it become a reality.

So what happened? The bronze plaques which explained the reason for the structure were stolen. They later turned up in Sterling and were sent to the Colorado Historical Society. That group refused to allow Kit Carson people to place them back on the monument for fear they might be stolen again. The Society made no effort to explain to motorists why that tower is a point of interest, much to the chagrin of the people who built it.

The Old Trails Monument. Photo by author

THE HAPPY PEOPLE OF TOONERVILLE

A Town Named for a Comic Strip

Toonerville still appears on Colorado maps, twenty-two miles south of Las Animas on State Highway 101. There is hardly anything left of the town which was economically blown away in the Dust Bowl of the 1930s.

According to the historian Perry Eberhart, the town was originally named Red Rock, and the farmers and ranchers gathered there weekends with their families to have fun together with baseball games, dances, rodeos, potluck suppers, and singing songs.

They decided that the name of Red Rock did not describe the happy times in those gatherings. Back when almost all comic strips were still comic, one of the favorites was named "The Toonerville Trolley" and the characters in it were usually playing funny jokes on each other. The Santa Fe Railroad had a line through the town, so the train came to be known as the Toonerville Trolley, and the people as Toonerville Folks.

Alas, the devastation of the winds which blew the good soil away and destroyed crops and homes with layers of dust caused many of the Toonerville people to pack up and move away.

DAUGHTERS OF THE MOON

Rare Butterflies in Unaweep Canyon

"By the shores of Gitche Gumee,
By the shining Big-Sea-Water,
Stood the wigwam of Nokomis,
Daughter of the Moon, Nokomis."

So begins Longfellow's famous narrative poem, "The Song of Hiawatha." Nokomis is both nurse and mentor to the child Hiawatha. It was after this woman that the rare butterfly, the Nokomis Fritillary, was named. Nokomis means "daughter of the moon." The male is a spectacular sight, with blazing orange wings nearly four inches across, and with silver spots on the underside.

Also known as the Great Basin Silver Spot, this lepidoptera breeds only in a few tiny selected places in the world, including one in southern Arizona and several in Nevada. It also has its home in what are called The Seeps in Unaweep Canyon, not far from the village of Gateway.

That is where a species of violets, *viola nephrophylla*, grows. The female Nokomis lays her eggs in that flower. When the larvae hatch from the eggs, they spend the winter among the dead weeds. As the violets bloom once more in the spring, they eat the leaves, form chrylases, and emerge in midsummer in all their magnificent glory. They are most abundant from mid-July until early September.

The Bureau of Land Management has preserved an eighty-acre reserve around what are also known as Unaweep Springs in order to protect the rare species. They have few natural enemies, but the ground-scratching towhee birds sometimes get a few of the larvae.

MORE ABOUT UNAWEEP CANYON

They Called It "Little Yosemite"

Some early explorers returning from California were so impressed by Unaweep Canyon's soaring cliffs that they compared it to the Yosemite Valley. It is now a part of the spectacular Unaweep-Tabeguache Scenic Byway, State Highway 141.

There are the narrows of Nine-Mile Hill, and the open valley above. Thimble Rock protrudes above the valley which gives a miniature version of the formation at Yosemite.

Unaweep Canyon is a geological oddity – one of the few canyons anywhere with streams running in opposite directions.

Along the roadside are the remains of Drigg's mansion. These consist arched stone relics of a fine home. It was stated by one reviewer that William Barrett was inspired to write his famous novel *Lilies of the Field* when he viewed these ruins. It later became the movie which won an Academy Award for Sidney Poitier.

Unaweep Canyon. Photo by author

ABOUT THE QUESTIONABLE BEHAVIOR

AND OUTRIGHT LAWLESSNESS

OUR SHAKY TERRITORIAL GOVERNANCE
Fudging, Bribery and Outright Graft

William Gilpin was named first governor of the Territory of Colorado in 1861 by President Abraham Lincoln. He lost his job as a result of having decided on his own that a volunteer infantry regiment was needed. Instead of petitioning the Federal Government for funds, he simply issued $375,000 in drafts on the U.S. Treasury. Although he claimed that Lincoln had implied he would back the drafts, the President ousted Gilpin and appointed John Evans to the gubernatorial post.

By that time Colorado had elected Hiram P. Bennet to be its first representative in the U.S. Congress. Bennet and Evans both fought hard for the establishment of a U.S. mint in Denver but there was no support in the House of Representatives until Bennet arranged for Thaddeus Stevens, Republican leader of that body, to receive a solid gold snuff box. The bribe worked. Later, Stevens was the leading promoter of the impeachment of President Andrew Johnson for being too soft on the South following the Civil War, charging corruption in office. Conviction failed by only one vote.

Evans was let go by Lincoln because of his implication in the Sand Creek Massacre of Cheyenne Indians who had been promised safe haven. Evans issued a pamphlet proclaiming his innocence, but it did not prevent his discharge.

During the succeeding terms of Alexander Cummings and A. Cameron Hunt, there were many charges of corruption but very little provable evidence. That was the era of political spoils in appointments, and officials were often accused of accepting bribes.

The administration of Ulysses Grant as President was one of considerable graft although some historians maintain that Grant knew little of what was going on. Among his appointees was Edward McCook as Colorado Governor. McCook manipulated a contract to deliver horses to the Ute Indians by having a relative get the winning bid at an inflated price. It was later proven that McCook himself was the one who made the most profit on the deal, some $22,000, with inferior horses being delivered. For that and some other charges, McCook was discharged.

He was followed by Samuel Elbert, Evans' son-in-law, but McCook and his supporters raised such a ruckus with the issue that Grant turned around, fired Elbert, and re-appointed McCook, one of the most unpopular men in the state. By this time, his own Republican Party had disowned McCook, and Grant was forced to remove him once more.

With all of this political upheaval it is little wonder that Colorado, which had sought statehood as early as 1861, never got that status until 1876.

Govener Edward McCook. Photo Courtesy P. David Smith

LEADVILLE'S FIRST "INVESTIGATIVE REPORTER"

And His Creative Imagination

Colorado has had a significant number of journalists who gained national fame. Some of them, in addition to serious reporting, would create stories from their own imagination if real news was lacking. Among these have been Denver's Eugene Field and Gene Fowler, Damon Runyan of both Pueblo and Denver, Ouray's David Day, and Cy Warman of Creede. One who had the same talents but never gained such a spot in popular history was Orth Stein of Leadville.

The editor who had hired him in 1880 thought Stein must have been delayed by a slow train when he didn't report for work on the assigned date. The son of an affluent Indiana family, Orth was hours overdue when he finally arrived in the office of the *Daily Chronicle* with a blockbuster of a story.

It seems he had arrived on time but spent most of the day calling on every medical doctor in the boomtown. He had posed as a medical student looking for a suitable professional with whom to learn more. This meant examining the qualifications of each physician. He had found a number of them had certificates from schools that never existed. Orth had "lifted" the diploma of one of them: it turned out to be a working card for a plasterers' union.

When the story was printed, a number of "doctors" had to close up shop in a hurry.

The new reporter added much to the *Chronicle's* circulation. When President Garfield was assassinated in 1881, Stein wrote regular articles on the tragedy. He noticed a rather quiet woman who would buy a copy each day and read these articles carefully. Upon confronting her, he found that she was the divorced wife of Charles Guiteau, the man who had killed Garfield.

That led to interviews and stories which made front page news throughout the nation. Almost overnight the newshound had become famous. This may have impressed him with his own ability, but there did not seem to be any more such sensational items for his pen.

He did get national attention again when he wrote of a spectacular, but secret, underground cavern which had been discovered near the town of Red Cliff. It was covered with crystals and gold, and an ancient sailing ship was floating in the underground pond. National magazines took up the account, and it was even featured in the popular **Crofutt's Grip Sack Guide to Colorado**, one of the books published for those who would seek their fortune in this state. The entire story was made up by Orth, but it kept his name as a reporter in the limelight.

Not willing to settle for that, he created a giant sea serpent which lived in Twin Lakes, and the discovery of a man's remains with chains fastened to a steel collar about the neck with bowls of food just beyond the reach of the victim. Newspapers in New York loved these shocking items and they were picked up worldwide.

When the reporter encountered legal troubles in the mining town, he left for Kansas City where he was arrested later for a murder. His family connections were such that he was able to beat the charge, and even then he robbed his mother of her jewelry. Eventually Orth Stein was seen living in corruption in New Orleans where he reportedly died of consumption.

Leadville in 1879. Colorado: Its Gold and Silver Mines

THE NUN WHO HELPED TAME TRINIDAD

Sister Blandina's Missions of Mercy

In 1872 the new town of Trinidad was one of the wildest in the West. On the frontier near New Mexico Territory, it was a hideout for numerous wanted men. Ranchers fought for grazing lands and the coal mines were subject to many conflicting claims. It was on December 9 of that year that Sister Blandina, age twenty-two, arrived to become a missionary teacher.

Born Rosa Maria Seagle, the nun had grown up in a very religious Italian home. She joined the Sisters of Charity and taught in the parochial schools at Steubenville, Ohio. It is said that she prayed to be sent to the Far West and that she was elated when assigned to go to Trinidad to open a school. The Sister took the railroad to the end of the line, then the town of Kit Carson, and proceeded by stagecoach to the wild town where she quickly befriended a number of the citizens.

It was later that she was secretly informed of a plot to murder the owner of a mine. Two employees knew they could take over a very profitable coal mine if the owner died. They set up false props in the tunnel designed to collapse when the owner went in the next day. Aghast at the idea, Sister Blandina persuaded an Indian friend to go out and get himself hired at the mine where he was to inspect and find the booby traps and repair them. Neither the owner of the mine nor the plotters knew that she had interfered with the scheme. It seems the Indian later revealed the details.

On another occasion, one of her students told her that the pupil's father was to be lynched for shooting a man who lay dying in the hospital. Sister Blandina went to see the victim and persuaded him to forgive his attacker. Then she went to the sheriff and asked that the jailed culprit be taken to the bedside of the man he shot to ask for forgiveness. Although he knew a lynch mob was forming, the sheriff finally acquiesced to the nun's plea. Thus the sheriff, the criminal, and the nun walked out into the main street of Trinidad toward the hospital. A mob followed them into the building. Claiming he had not realized what an awful thing he had done, the prisoner asked for and was given forgiveness. That was overheard by the angry mob which then permitted a lawful trial, the accused man being sentenced to prison. Many believed that ended mob rule in Trinidad.

There were no other witnesses to this subsequent incident, but we have the nun's own account to believe. Two followers of the notorious William Bonney, better known as Billy the Kid, happened to be at Dick Wooten's toll gate atop Raton Pass when they had a falling-out. Both of the vicious gunslingers drew at the same time. One was killed; the other critically wounded.

The survivor was brought to Trinidad and left in an abandoned adobe hut to die. The four physicians in town refused to treat the outlaw. Sister Blandina, with two of her friends for protection, went to the victim with food and medication to treat the wound. She returned several times over the course of three weeks, but the patient became weaker. He told her that Bonney was coming the next day to kill the four doctors for refusing treatment.

The woman of the cloth came the next day to face Billy the Kid herself. He was very grateful for the help she had given and offered to do her any favor she asked. When she asked that he not murder the doctors, according to the account, he was true to his word and left town. The medical men were never told that their lives had been threatened.

Later serving in Santa Fe, it is not known what other merciful acts she may have performed. After twenty-one years on the frontier she was recalled to Cincinnati to work among the Italian community there. She lived to be ninety-one years old.

Early postcard view of Tridad, Colorado
Photo Courtesy P. David Smith

GERMAN PRISONERS OF WAR IN COLORADO

And the Escape from Camp Hale

During World War II there were at least three German prisoner of war camps in Colorado. Unlike the horror stories of American soldiers who were imprisoned in German camps, conditions at Trinidad, Colorado Springs, and Greeley were reportedly good. Prisoners given work assignments were actually paid and could purchase candy bars, cigarettes, and other items which were not on the standard supply lists.

Detachments from the Greeley camp worked in the sugar beet fields to replace the laborers who had gone off to war. While they were supplied with a sandwich in the field, often the farmers' wives would cook them good meals. This practice was at least frowned upon by the Army guards.

Some of the prisoners were sent into the mountains to work to help in cutting trees and work in the lumber mill at Walden. Citizens who drove them between the towns commented on the fact that the Germans had an ample supply of candy and other items which were very hard to obtain on the civilian market.

At Fraser there was another POW camp for timber cutting. The prisoners cut ice for railroad refrigerator cars at Kremmling. There were very few attempts to escape. This inland and mountainous region might be so far away from the sea that such attempts were useless but it was the duty of a prisoner to try to escape. Some who did walk off were almost happy to be recaptured and given warm quarters and adequate food.

There was one exception to those attempts: the great escape of two prisoners from Camp Hale, the training camp of the Tenth Mountain Division near Leadville. A detachment from the Trinidad compound was stationed there to help in maintenance and other tasks.

In the same camp was the 620th Engineer General Service Company. An American unit composed of soldiers who were considered pro-Nazi or pro-Fascist in their views. They were also kept away from the chance to desert with assignments deep inland.

Among the men in the Army unit was a brilliant young man, PFC Dale H. Maple. He had been a prodigy as a youth and graduated *magna cum laude* from Harvard University. Not only did he have a vast knowledge of music, history, and geography, but he was fluent in twenty-six foreign languages! Maple admired Adolf Hitler and even tried to get the German embassy to take him with them when the U.S. declared war on that nation. Aware of this attempt, the military assigned him to the Engineer Unit.

Perhaps the security was not very good at Camp Hale, but some of the engineers struck up an acquaintance with the prisoners. Maple devised a scheme to take two Nazi soldiers to Mexico with him so that they would all be able to escape to Germany.

Taking a bus from Camp Hale to Salida, Maple bought supplies and a used car for which he paid $255. Concealing these at the town of Red Cliff, on February 15, 1944, he was able to retrieve the car and pick up the two Germans. The trio drove southward to Alamosa, then through New Mexico, when their 1934 Reo had a flat with no spare tire. Riding the rim, the escapees finally drove into a ditch and had to begin walking.

They hiked with their packsacks into Mexico. It was there that a peon guiding a horse and wagon encountered them and notified Mexican police who took them to Columbus, New Mexico. There they were identified and the two Germans returned to Trinidad.

Maple was tried for treason by a Court-Martial and was sentenced to death despite his eloquent 7,000-word statement. Upon the advice of the Army's judge advocate general, President Roosevelt commuted the sentence to life imprisonment, and his sentence was later reduced to ten years after which he was released in 1951.

WHEN COLORADO WAS BLOCKADED

No Poor People Allowed In

In 1936 during the depth of the so-called Great Depression, unemployment was rampant in Colorado. Although farmers had long depended on transient workers from Mexico and New Mexico to help cultivate and harvest crops, there was much racial prejudice brought on by the fact that these workers would expect less pay than others in those jobs. The prejudice even extended to Hispanics who had lived in Colorado for generations.

It was on April 18 that year that the governor, "Big Ed" Johnson, declared a blockade of the southern border of the state. No aliens were to be allowed over the state line. Americans who did not have enough money with them were also sent back. Colorado National Guard troops were called in to establish check points at Campo, south of Springfield, Trinidad, Conejos, and Durango.

All vehicles were ordered to stop. If anyone could not show enough money or if there was anyone who was not an American citizen, the transient was not allowed into the state. The first truckload at the Trinidad entrance to be turned back had only three dollars altogether. Some others could only show thirty cents. One woman who looked impoverished was ordered to return home until she showed them that she carried $5,000!

The troops stayed at such fine hostelries as the Columbian Hotel in Trinidad and the famous Strater in Durango.

The *Denver Post* enthusiastically supported this idea, but the *Rocky Mountain News* felt it was a seriously questionable policy. Railroad trains from New Mexico were also stopped, and hobos were sent walking back to Raton. Johnson boasted that he had saved a thousand jobs for Colorado residents. After about 400 had been rejected, the migrants seem to have given up trying to enter by that route.

Johnson proclaimed that if Colorado continued to be overrun by "wandering job thieves" he would close the other three borders to the state. The governor of New Mexico demanded an explanation as many rejected travelers were U.S. citizens. As many raised constitutional questions regarding the blockade, the martial law was stopped on April 30, two weeks after it had begun.

It is ironic to think that only a few years later during World War II, Governor Ralph Carr defied a national ruling placing Japanese Americans in internment camps. He welcomed those from the west coast to come and live in Colorado and refused state cooperation in evacuating the targeted race. However he could not keep the Feds from establishing an internment camp at Amity in southeastern Colorado.

AN INMATE PRAISES THE STATE PENITENTIARY

"Most Valuable Year" of the Doctor's Life

In Issue Two of *Colorado Heritage* in 1987, there was reprinted a story which had appeared in a short-lived Denver publication in 1893. It was written by Dr. T. Thatcher Graves who was an inmate sentenced to hang for the murder of a prominent Boston widow.

Although the evidence was mostly circumstantial, it seems the victim had drunk from a bottle of whiskey laced with arsenic which had been sent her by the doctor. The physician had hoped to profit from her will. Found guilty and given the death sentence, he had won an appeal for a second trial, but in the meantime he was sentenced to the prison at Cañon City.

In that article Graves praised the location as one of the "most beautiful and attractive places in the Western World." Although the inmates were among the most vicious to be found anywhere, they were being reformed, learning many trades by which they could pursue constructive lives thanks to the orderly and capable staff of the institution.

He described the brick-making, construction skills, and other vocational programs. As to the tailor shop he wrote, "Happy is the 'Con' who is so fortunate" as to be assigned there where the art of mending would astonish the layman.

Graves was convinced that the State Prison of Colorado was superior "in every respect" to that of any other penal institution in the nation.

After maintaining that his year there had been the most valuable of his life, he felt dedicated to a new mission. That was to learn if any of those incarcerated were innocent men. If he found one he would "hammer at the gate." giving no rest or peace to the society "until the grated doors fly wide open and the rescued walks forth among his fellow men."

Editor Judith Gamble, doing further research, learned that Dr. Graves had been transferred to the Arapahoe County Jail for re-trial. There, the night before his hearing, he committed suicide. Nine years later a suicide note was released claiming he had been haunted by the ghost of the woman he was accused of murdering.

State Penitentiary at Cañon City Photo Courtesy P. David Smith

COLORADO'S SPECTACULAR SUBMERGED CITY

Another Good Story Dashed!

No one is sure when the account first appeared, but it was in an insurance brochure many years ago and in an American Legion publication as recently as the 1960s.

Somewhere near Silver Plume was a lake, possibly Green Lake or Blue Lake. It was once the site of a mining town. There was a gap in the mountains surrounding it, and a river flowed through that opening. When a landslide occurred, it dammed the river, flooding the town and creating the lake.

If a person were to take a boat out on the lake, he or she could look down and see the entire town: streets, church spires, houses, and even a locomotive in the station.

Historians Francis B. Rizzari and Robert L. Brown decided finally that this mythical story had to be ended. They pointed out that both of the lakes were there long before there was any mining or other occupation of the region. An earlier town, Brownsville, about a mile from Silver Plume, had once existed, but it was covered by a landslide.

There was no lake. That may have inspired some creative promoter to invent the tale.

SCRAPPING THE GREAT WALL OF CHINA

Could Denver Reporters Have Started a War?

According to four Denver newspapers on Sunday, June 25, 1899, four engineers had stopped over in the mile-high city on their way to China. They had been employed by a group of American millionaires to estimate the cost of tearing down the ancient Great Wall of China!

Started in about 214 B.C. by the vainglorious Chinese emperor Shih Huang Ti, the wall is 1,400 miles long, twenty feet high, and from eighteen to thirty feet in width. It was built by slaves, prisoners, and coolies. The idea was to keep northern invaders out of China.

It would appear that the millionaires had been asked by the then-current ruling family of China to plan the removal of the wall as an invitation to foreign trade, and to make space for a highway across the distance. This was a time when a Chinese secret society, the "Righteous and Harmonious Fists," more popularly known in the West as the "Boxers," were planning a drive to get rid of all "foreign devils," European and American missionaries and industrialists who were exploiting the resources of China. A rebellion was threatened.

There were four daily newspapers in Denver at that time: the *Republican*, the *Denver Times*, the *Denver Post*, and the *Rocky Mountain News*. The Oxford Hotel lounge was a popular meeting place for reporters in those days. On the Saturday night before this story appeared, it seems that there were newsmen from all four papers having drinks at the Oxford, and lamenting the lack of any exciting news. It was then that they concocted the story of the destruction of the China Wall. It was essential that the story appear in all the newspapers, to make it appear authentic. Each reporter then retired to write up his own version of the purported interview with the engineers.

That was such a great story that it was picked up by other newspapers throughout the nation and then the world!

Soon after the story came out, the Boxer Rebellion erupted, and was quelled by European and American troops invading China. Many lives, mostly Chinese, were lost, and that empire was subjected to gross humiliation and heavy reparations.

A year later a Methodist Bishop returned to Denver from a tour in China and conjectured that the uprising was touched off by the news that the Great Wall of China was to be destroyed by foreigners. There is probably no validity in this comment as the seeds of rebellion were already under way at the time that the Chinese newspapers carried the story.

Thus did a mere hoax to excite the Denver readers get out of hand.

PRAYING WITH A NOOSE AROUND HIS NECK

Happier With Jesus Than With Leadville

Leadville must have been one of the most lawless cities in the world in 1879 and 1880. It was teeming with all sorts of thieves and murderers as it had become almost overnight the second largest city in Colorado. Most of the crimes went unpunished, but the report of one is noteworthy.

Someone had stolen the silver from inside the Grand Hotel and then a horse from the front. A man was soon seen with the animal and the bag of silver, and the citizens decided to hang him at once. The reporter for the *Chronicle* later reported what happened. It should be noted that the reporter could not have remembered every word spoken, so he may have done some considerable tampering with the account.

It seems the miscreant claimed innocence saying he was merely keeping a sack and a horse that had been entrusted to him by a friend. He would not name the friend, even when the mob had tied a noose around his neck.

An early day lynching. From Hands Up, *1897*

They hoisted him up a few feet to give him the feel of his situation, and asked him again to name the culprit. He asked if he could have a moment to pray. After thanking God for His blessings and asking permission to enter Heaven, the account claimed, he added "Lord, you know that I didn't steal the horse and the things for which I am about to die. So You will forgive, won't You, good Lord, and let one of the angels come down and take me to heaven? Oh, if You will, it won't hurt much to die. I would a thousand times rather be with You and Jesus in Heaven than stay in Leadville any longer. Let me know, Lord, that I can come and I'll die like a Christian."

That prayer was so moving that a miner threatened to kill anyone who continued with the hanging, demanding the accused man have a fair trial. Still claiming innocence, the poor victim of this attempted lynching was taken to jail.

After a week or so there was a trial, and the prayerful one was found guilty. What never was revealed is what punishment was then given to him...it was never reported.

Newspapers were quite free-wheeling in those days, and perhaps this was all concocted by the reporter. Anyway, it's a good story, except for the ending.

An early adventure book, 1896. Author's collection

MEAN MEN IN OLD JULESBURG

Jules Beni, Jack Slade and "Blacksnake" Lachut

When Mark Twain got off the stage coach in Julesburg on a trip West, he described it as "the strangest, quaintest, funniest frontier town that our traveled eyes had ever stared at and been astonished by." Another traveler simply called it "the wickedest little city east of the Rockies."

Actually, there were four places named Julesburg, but they are all embraced by the area of the modern city of that name in the northeastern corner of Colorado. It was first a trail division in the gold rush of 1858. It was an important station on the Pony Express. Then it was a major transfer point for Ben Holladay's famous freight line. When the Union Pacific Railroad built a branch to Denver, the days of notoriety had departed, and Julesburg developed into a pleasant agricultural community.

Jules Beni is the one who called the town after himself; it had earlier been known as Overland City. Beni was Holladay's agent, but he was also considered a troubling dictator of the community. He was believed to be involved with Indians who raided nearby ranches. Holladay decided to fire him and employ a tough gunslinger named Jack Slade.

When Slade took over as stationmaster, Beni was very bitter, to say the least. Jules was suspected of stealing horses from the company. When Slade came to investigate, Beni fired two shots point blank into the manager. Then he triggered three more into the fallen man and ordered bystanders to bury the body. Instead, they ran Beni out of town. By what must have bordered on a miracle, Slade survived. It took a long time for him to recover but he swore he would track down Beni and cut off his ears.

In the meantime, Slade built Virginia Dale, a stage stop in the far north of Larimer County, naming it after his wife. Slade had a number of followers who tracked down Beni somewhere in that region and captured him.

When Jack arrived, he had Jules tied to a fence post where he proceeded to shoot the man in the legs and arms. When Beni finally died, Slade cut off his ears, according to the legend, nailed one to the post, and kept the other to wear on his watch chain.

An alcoholic, Slade was constantly getting in trouble when he was drunk. He nearly killed a man in Wyoming and had to escape to Montana. There, in 1864, he tore up the town and attempted to kidnap the judge. The vigilantes hanged him. Virginia swore she would not let him be buried in Montana, so she had the coffin lined with tin and filled with raw alcohol with the corpse sealed in. When the road to Salt Lake City had been cleared of snow three months later, she took a stage, with the coffin tied on top. She interred the body in an unmarked grave in the old section of the Salt Lake City cemetery.

Of course there were other rough characters in the days of Old Julesburg. One of the worst was a teamster known only as "Blacksnake" Lachut, who arrived in 1867. A master of profane language, he was even more adept with the accuracy of his whip and loved to scare people. He would lash the cigars out of bystanders' mouths and could break the necks of bottles from a bar across the room. One of his delights was to flick off the decorative buckle that supported the single strap of a dancing girl.

When a drunken man jostled him, Lachut hurled the lash that coiled around the man's neck and dragged the victim through the streets before then whipping the body to ribbons. No one would take this bully on, but he finally left town in 1870, much to the relief of everybody.

SECRET EXECUTION OF THE
NOTORIOUS REYNOLDS GANG

Bones Bleaching on the Prairie

Alston Knox Shaw was about fifty-five years old in the 1880s when he bought a ranch near Juanita, a mining town later named Bowie, upriver from Paonia. That was when he told a story solving a question that had baffled historians for more than two decades.

It seems that Shaw was a member of the Third Colorado Volunteers during the Civil War. This unit later gained infamy in the Sand Creek Massacre of several hundred Cheyenne Indians in southeastern Colorado. However, the participants considered that massacre either a Civil War battle or a justifiable revenge against Indians in general.

Early in that war, one James Reynolds, who had been a prospector at Oro City near what became Leadville, returned to his native Texas to raise a rebel gang. These men probably never did anything for the Confederate cause, but they did raid wagon trains and stagecoaches claiming they were conducting war raids. In the process, they killed a number of victims and were considered a notorious outlaw gang.

One of their hold-ups was atop Kenosha Pass near Fairplay. They reputedly looted $75,000 in gold, $100,000 in currency, and "a considerable haul in diamonds" in that one raid. If later information is to be believed, they buried the bounty at a marked spot in Handcart Gulch, about ten miles northwest of the town of Grant.

In due time, some of the members were caught; others escaped and later left tales or even maps as to where the treasure was buried. Reynolds himself was wounded and when he sought help, he and four companions were captured. After a quick trial at Buckskin Joe, a mining camp above Fairplay, they were taken to Denver.

While Denver was dedicated to the Union cause, there were many Confederate sympathizers in that town. It was decided that there might be violence if the gang members were executed in the capital city. It became the duty of a unit of the Third Volunteers to accompany the prisoners to Fort Lyon, on the Arkansas River, and thence to Fort Leavenworth, Kansas, to face a firing squad.

Apparently on that route, several soldiers were placed on guard at each camp. When it became Shaw's turn, he was given the duty three nights in a row and complained to his commander that he should not have to watch over the gang members every night. Shaw stated that he would just as soon shoot them.

Captain Cree then explained that the scheme of sending them all the way to Fort Leavenworth was simply a bluff. The prisoners were supposed to "try to escape" somewhere along the way. It seems that the Reynolds gang had sworn to stay together "until their bones bleached the prairie." Shaw and some other soldiers took the ambulance behind a nearby butte one afternoon. There he told the gang to line up, and reminded them of their sworn obligation.

Shaw showed them a copy of orders for their execution and asked if they had any messages to send to relatives. The prisoners replied that they wanted no one to know what had happened.

At that, all five were faced with a firing squad. Shaw placed a blank cartridge in one rifle before ordering the soldiers to kill the bandits. Reynolds appeared quite brave, but one of his cohorts pled that he had never killed anyone. Shaw then reminded him that he was in bad company and gave the order to fire. After the men fell, each was given an additional bullet through the head from Shaw's revolver. Handcuffs and leg irons were removed, and the leader addressed the corpses: "We will leave you free to fulfill the last of your obligations, to stick together while your bones bleach on the prairie."

When the executioners returned to the main unit, Captain Cree asked what had happened. Shaw replied that the soldiers had stopped to dig some potatoes, and the prisoners had escaped into the brush and were never found.

There were many rumors later circulated about skeletons being seen with bullet holes through the skulls, but it was not until twenty years later that this account came out.

ABOUT
DISASTROUS
EVENTS

THE HASTINGS HOLOCAUST

"Fire Damp" in the Coal Mine

There have been a number of disasters in Colorado mines. Probably the worst of all, according to the number of deaths, took place at the Hastings Coal Mine in Las Animas County on April 27, 1917.

There were 121 men who entered the mine that morning. None would leave the excavation alive. One of the great threats to coal mining was that of methane gas, also known as "fire damp," which could explode when ignited by flame. Miners had been equipped with electric helmet lights to prevent such a disaster, and some workers carried instruments to test for such gas.

Whether the detectors worked properly was not known. The gas is created by organic decomposition of coal. How had it been ignited? There was no great sound to be heard. One author compared the holocaust as being similar to touching a fire to gasoline in the open air in which there is no great noise but massive "whoo-oosh" sound. Coal dust may have added to the fire.

At 9:00 a.m., smoke came pouring from the portal. Days of search recovered all the bodies, burned beyond recognition. While the mine continued to operate after that, it closed in 1922, and the town of Hastings, with a population of 2,000, has disappeared.

Victims of an explosion at a Crested Butte Mine. Harpers Weekly *Febuary 16, 1884*

THE BRIDGE THAT FAILED

The Twentieth Century's Deadliest Single Train Crash

On August 7, 1904, a combination Denver and Rio Grande and Missouri Pacific excursion train was speeding southward to Pueblo from Denver. There were about 150 passengers aboard. Some were returning to homes in Pueblo; others would continue to the World's Fair in St. Louis.

About eight miles north of Pueblo was the town of Eden where the Fountain River flowed toward the Arkansas River. The engineer had been warned to slow as the train crossed the bridge over the creek there because the heavy rain had been falling in the headwaters of that stream.

As the locomotive crossed the bridge, it made the span safely, but then the structure collapsed, drawing the engine back into the flooded waters, and plunging all but the last three cars into the deluge. It was about 8:15 p.m. when the disaster occurred.

The engine itself was swept downstream and half buried in the sands. Rescue teams came from Pueblo and they and other volunteers worked all night trying to find survivors. Most of the passengers had been carried downstream. Efforts to find the bodies lasted for more than a week. Unfortunately, some of the many sightseers found purses and handbags, stealing the money and valuables from them.

Investigation proved the catastrophic event was an "act of nature." The railroad was not held responsible.

A total of ninety-six people were killed in the accident. Many others were injured. At least twenty-six were safe in the last three cars.

That accident had the most fatalities of any crash of a single train in twentieth century America. In 1910 two trains were plunged into a canyon in an avalanche near Wellington, Washington, resulting in ninety-six fatalities. In 1918 two trains collided near Nashville, Tennessee, killing 101.

A CALAMITOUS HARVEST FESTIVAL

The Air Show Crash at Flagler

The town of Flagler is about 120 miles southeast of Denver, in the heart of Colorado's Great Plains. A center for grain production, it carried on a yearly Harvest Festival every September. The town had a rich tradition, perhaps best described by the famous writer, Hal Borland, who grew up there, in his book **County Editor's Boy**.

In 1951 the celebration on Saturday, September 15, was to include an airshow performed by a Denver company which specialized in such events. After a morning parade and various contests, farmers and ranchers from miles around joined the citizenry of Flagler to see the wonders to be performed by aviators.

There was no stadium as such. People parked their cars around the football field which would be the main viewing point.

Among the most spectacular stunts was to be a diving plane spouting smoke from a skywriting generator. It was piloted by an Air Force officer who had flown in World War II, twenty-nine-year-old Norman Jones.

At a speed reaching 110 miles per hour, the aircraft came into sight and then began a barrel roll, spouting the smoke. Down it came, to the thrills of the viewers, but when it was upside down and only 150 feet above the field, terror took over. Unable to correct, Jones crashed into the rows of cars.

Carnage was everywhere. Smashed automobiles and parts of the plane flew through the air. Nineteen people were killed and another thirty were injured, some seriously. Doctors, nurses, and morticians from many miles around rushed to the scene to help as best they could, but the disaster would remain in the hearts of the citizens forever.

Of course the pilot was killed so no one knew for certain what had happened in a stunt he had performed in previous shows. Investigators listed it as pilot error; others felt that Jones had wanted to try something a bit more daring than before.

A memorial listing the names of the victims serves as a reminder of that horrible day.

Memorial to crash victims at Fowler. Photo by author

BENEVOLENT BEQUESTS

A Tragic Story of Cannibalism on the Plains

Five men from Illinois joined a party headed for the Pike's Peak Gold Rush. Setting out in February of 1859, three brothers, Alexander, Daniel, and Charles Blue, a cousin, John Campbell, and one Thomas Stevenson joined a party led by John Gibbs taking the Smoky Hill Trail to the gold fields.

A terrible storm stopped the party as they journeyed across what is now western Kansas. After nine days the Gibbs group decided to stop and hunt for buffalo to sustain their rations. The original Blue party of five, plus a man named George Soley, disagreed, believing they would do better to reach Denver sooner.

The six men, without a compass or tent, left to follow what they thought was the trail but soon encountered another raging storm. Hoping to be guided by the sun, they realized that the sun didn't appear for days on end. They thought they were only about fifty-five miles from Denver but were probably some 170 miles away in what is now Cheyenne County.

They ate a dog that had followed them and did shoot a few rabbits, but then they grew weaker and weaker. Campbell and Stevenson set off to try to find help. It was by that time that the sojourners realized they had been traveling in a circle.

Soley was very ill, and when he realized he was going to die, he told the others they should eat of his body rather than to starve. After three days, the survivors, horrified by their act, did cut into the corpse and eat. Although this helped a little, Alexander Blue knew he would not live and asked his brothers to partake of his body, too.

Daniel and Charles continued in what they now thought was the right direction as a mountain, probably Pike's Peak, had been sighted on the western horizon. Charles couldn't make it and died. Daniel, now alone, lay down in agony, but after three days, he also ate part of his brother Charles' body.

Daniel fell unconscious. The next thing he knew, he had been found by some Arapahoe Indians and taken to their camp where he was given antelope meat and blood.

Two days later he could sit up. The Indians took him to the station of the Pike's Peak Overland Express Company where he boarded a stage for Denver.

Heart-broken and disillusioned with the prospects of gold, he returned to Illinois where he wrote up the details of the ill-fated journey.

Nothing was known by Daniel Blue as to what became of Campbell and Stevenson.

Pike's Peakers returning home. Harpers Weekly *August 13, 1859*

AN AVALANCHE AT TWIN LAKES

And Its Canine Survivor

The hamlet of Twin Lakes is a beautiful place named for the lakes beside it. It lies beneath Parry Peak, a shoulder of Mount Elbert, the state's highest elevation. The town of Twin Lakes is seventeen miles south of Leadville.

As the second of two very heavy snowfalls descended on the village, perhaps some citizen was reading about the avalanche which is now regarded as the most costly in human lives ever known. It had thundered down the side of Mount Huascarn in the Peruvian Andes, killing more than 3,000 people on January 10, 1962. Snow was still falling on January 20 above Twin Lakes ten days after that, and some of the people there were beginning to wonder if such a snowslide could hit them.

At about 5:30 the next morning, a Sunday, the avalanche came roaring down Gordon Gulch at the edge of town completely destroying two homes and damaging nearby buildings. In the first house covered, General (that was his first name) Sheldon, his wife, son, and two daughters were killed. Across the road was the home of Bill and Barbara Adamish. They and their two sons lived there, along with their dog, Pepe, who was pregnant and had taken to staying indoors under the kitchen table.

Rescuers were able to rescue both Bill and Barbara after some hours. Both had survived only because they had been thrown into peculiar positions with pockets of air. Also rescued was Pepe, a mixture of terrier, Pekinese and bulldog, who was found under the crushed table. Only later did they find the bodies of the two Adamish sons.

A week after the avalanche, Pepe, now taken to Leadville, gave birth to seven puppies. As part of a community effort which raised $7,000 in aid for the stricken families, the puppies were auctioned off.

THE TRAGEDY ON MOUNT BETHEL

Football Special Flight Ended in Tragedy

As a motorist approaches the East Portal of the Eisenhower Tunnel driving west on Interstate Highway 70, Mount Bethel, 12,075 feet in elevation, towers on the north of the road. About ten miles up from Georgetown, this mountain was the site of a disastrous air crash on October 2, 1970.

The football team of Wichita State University, Kansas, had chartered two twin-engine Martin 404 aircraft to fly to Logan, Utah for a game with Utah State University. After a stop in Denver, one of the planes flew northward to Wyoming to continue the flight. The other decided to cross the Continental Divide in Colorado, following the route of the interstate highway then under construction.

There were forty-one aboard, including twenty-two football players, officials of the college, prominent supporters, and some of their wives. As the craft approached the construction site of the Eisenhower tunnel, it became evident that it did not have the lifting power to cross the Divide.

It was then decided to circle and return to Denver. The co-pilot began a sharp turn to the left. The pilot took control and steered to the right, slowing the plane to a stall over a box canyon on the mountain and a sharp fall. Because of the slow speed, a few survived the crash and the fire which erupted.

Workers at the tunnel site rushed to rescue those who could be saved. Fire departments from Idaho Springs and Georgetown arrived to try to control the blaze and search for survivors. The death toll eventually reached thirty-one.

Investigation proved the airplane was overloaded and did not have the lifting power to cross the mountains.

A memorial marker has been placed beside the highway near the disaster site, and another one stands on the University campus in Wichita to commemorate the calamity.

TWO HORRIBLE SCHOOL BUS CALAMITIES

Towner and Gunnison

A great blizzard struck the area of Towner, two miles from the Kansas state line in Kiowa County, on Thursday, March 26, 1931. When school bus driver Carl Miller brought twenty children to the Pleasant Hill schoolhouse that morning it was decided the storm was so bad school would be dismissed that day and the children returned to their homes.

Miller decided to save time by taking a short cut over an abandoned road. Only a mile from the school, visibility was impossible, and the bus veered off the road. The crash broke three windows of the bus and damaged the motor so that it could not be started again. The driver finally decided to go for help. Lost in the driven snow, he collapsed and died three miles away from the bus.

In attempts to stay warm, the children burned schoolbooks and anything else they could find on the vehicle. It was not until 6:30 the next evening that searchers located the bus. A boy by the name of Bryan Untied had been keeping the children moving and had used his own coat to keep some of them warm. In spite of his efforts, five of the children died.

Untied became a hero throughout the nation. He was the personal guest of President Herbert Hoover late the next month. The sad fate of the victims will never be forgotten.

On Saturday, September 11, 1971, a school bus from Gunnison was headed over Monarch Pass on the Continental Divide. There were forty-eight people aboard including the Gunnison Junior High School football team bound for a game in Salida and several adults including the driver.

Atop the pass, the driver attempted to shift gears for the east side downhill drive. Suddenly neither the brakes nor the gearshift worked, and the bus careened down the highway. It was amazing that it got as far as it did. At the village of Garfield, 6.3 miles below the summit, it veered off and rolled two and a half times ejecting thirty-nine of the passengers.

Eight players and their coach were either killed by impact or crushed as the roof of the bus collapsed. MAST military helicopters were rushed to the site of the accident and took fifteen of the wounded to St. Luke's Hospital in Denver. Most survivors were injured, some very critically.

Severely hurt and in traumatic shock, the driver was never able to recall the disastrous events preceding the crash.

A federal investigation placed the blame on a defective braking system in the bus which was a new one in the school's fleet. The report also cited the weak structure of the sides and roof of the bus, as well as the "unforgiving nature of the road terrain."

The investigation led to many improved standards for the construction of buses designed for mountain travel, and a runaway truck ramp was added to that stretch of highway which had in five years experienced 111 accidents and five fatalities in addition to the bus tragedy.

NOT-TO-BE-FORGOTTEN DISASTERS

A Chronicle of the Worst

The greatest hotel fire in Colorado history was the explosion of the steam plant in the Gumry Hotel in Denver on August 19, 1895. Twenty-two people including the owner were killed; an estimated forty-two survived but some were injured for life.

A flood of the Arkansas River on June 3, 1921, caused more than a hundred deaths in Pueblo and other places downstream. Six hundred homes were destroyed.

On July 31, 1976, the eve of Colorado's centennial, a flash flood swept down the canyon of the Big Thompson River above the city of Loveland. There were 145 people known dead, and six more of the missing have never been found and were presumed to have been killed.

The greatest killer of all was the worldwide influenza pandemic of 1918-19. It is estimated that between 5,000 and 5,500 Coloradans succumbed to the flu or resulting pneumonia.

As this work is primarily concerned with lesser-known events, little attention is paid to those which have received detailed treatment elsewhere. Nevertheless, the following should also never be forgotten.

On November 29, 1864, at Sand Creek, the Colorado Third Volunteers massacred possibly 150 mostly unarmed Cheyenne Indians who already had raised the white flag of surrender.

John Graham planted a bomb in his mother's luggage on November 1, 1955. It exploded in flight, killing all forty-four aboard. This was the greatest air disaster in Colorado

The most publicized of all was the horrible killing of fellow students and a teacher at Columbine High School in Littleton on April 20, 1999. These murders have become a worldwide horror story of youth violence.

Fourteen fire fighters were killed in a catastrophic forest fire at Storm King Mountain near Glenwood Springs on July 6, 1994. It was the deadliest forest fire in the history of the state.

ABOUT THE QUEEN CITY

THAT MAN ATOP THE PIONEER MONUMENT

No One Cared to Ask What the Navajo Thought

It was decided in 1906 to build a Pioneer Monument at the corner of Broadway and Colfax in Denver, the end of the historic "59ers" Smoky Hill Trail. Sculptor Frederick MacMonnies was given the commission.

A model of the monument showed a miner, a trapper, and a pioneer mother at the base but topped with a heroic sculpture of an Indian. Denverites were outraged, and claimed that the Indian did not belong. They demanded that the top figure be replaced by their most popular hero, Christopher "Kit" Carson.

Kit Carson has been one of the most celebrated scouts in the history of the West. Towns, cities, counties, mountains and even a national forest have been named for him. To the Navajo Indians, he is what Adolf Eichman is to the Jews.

Carson had, indeed, compiled a remarkable record as a great scout. He had negotiated with various Indian tribes in fairness and even had an Indian wife at one time. When the Civil War broke out, the Union Army became concerned that the South would try to take over New Mexico and Arizona cutting off what might be sources of gold to finance the North.

It was then that this army, whose Commander-in-Chief was, of course, President Abraham Lincoln, commissioned Carson to round up the Navajos and march them hundreds of miles to a reservation 165 miles southwest of Santa Fe, New Mexico. The scout enlisted the help of the Ute Indians, telling them that every Navajo they could capture might be kept as a slave or sold as a slave to Mexican farmers – this edict issued by the army of the man who would become known as "The Great Emancipator!"

With many Navajo being killed outright, Carson was successful in rounding up the rest and sending them on what has become known as "The Long Walk," a Southwest equivalent to the infamous "Trail of Tears." Evicted from the lands they felt had been given to them by divine sources, the Navajo prisoners were forced to walk all the way across New Mexico, with many deaths on the way.

When they reached the destination, Bosque Redondo, they were forced into slave labor to become farmers of the unproductive soil. Many became ill; some women were seduced by their captors. The government failed to supply enough food to give the Indians needed nourishment and many died. It was not until 1868, after many shocking investigations, that they were allowed to return to their homeland.

For his service, Carson was given command of Fort Garland in Colorado, his last great assignment.

Atop the monument in Denver, Carson sits on a horse as an immortal hero.

The Man atop Pioneer Monuent. Photo by Randy Fay

PLANS TO MAKE DENVER A SEAPORT

Dreams of Thirty-Seven Ocean-Going Steamers

No one seems to have heard of F.E. Atitstill before or since his moment in the *Denver Republican* newspaper October 22, 1904. That publication had a reputation for straight news, unlike some of the other Denver dailies. That is why an interview with Atitstill might have been considered seriously.

The plans, according to the interview, were to dredge the Mississippi and Missouri Rivers and then the Platte and South Platte clear to Denver. The entrepreneur had already purchased five blocks along Cherry Creek to dock the ships, he claimed.

His plans were to buy thirty-seven ocean freighters to bring fruit to Colorado at a lower cost and to ship hay to England at a much lower price.

Among his other boasts were that he had already purchased the Union Pacific and Southern Pacific Railroads to connect with the West Coast. Somewhere along there, it would seem that the reporter would have raised an eyebrow regarding these extravagant claims.

Nevertheless, the story made it over the editorial desk and proved to be a sensational newsbreak. There was no follow-up.

The Colorado State Capital building. Courtesy P. David Smith

WHITHER THE CAPITOL BUILDING?

At Least a Dozen Communities Sought It

While Denver had been the center of the Territorial Government of Colorado, there was no provision that it would continue as such once statehood had been achieved in 1876.

By 1881 plans were being made to actually build a capitol building. The state legislative body was, under the constitution, to designate the location. In the meantime, Denver would continue its function.

Once the question was raised in 1880, fur began to fly. Leadville, then the second largest city in the state, pointed out that it was more centrally located and was the most economically productive community. It had already established a "Capitol Hill." When the State General Assembly decided that there must be an election of the people to decide the issue, a vote was set for November 8, 1881.

In addition to Denver and Leadville, other towns jumped in as candidates: Pueblo, Colorado Springs, Canon City, Salida, Golden, Gunnison, Greeley, and Hot Sulphur Springs. Trinidad and Central City put in their own bids before the election.

Denver was the winner with almost two thirds of the votes: 30,248. In second place was Pueblo, with 6,047; third was Colorado Springs, 4,700; Canon City won 2,788, and Salida came in with 695. The other candidates had a total of 929 votes.

That should have settled the matter, but several contestants wanted another election as the decade progressed.

Gunnison later was bitter about the outcome as the granite for the Capitol Building came from a nearby quarry and the city pointed out the great savings that could have been realized if the structure were put up on Smelter Hill there. Generally, though, the lawmakers did not even consider moving to such a cold place. Leadville had its own Capitol Hill, but with its elevation of over 10,200 feet, it was never able to persuade legislators that a new election should be held before actual construction of the statehouse was begun in Denver.

DENVER'S TOWN CRIER

Beloved Old Lige

Elijah Wentworth was born a slave in Virginia. He never was sure how old he was, but he must have been middle-aged when he arrived in Denver in 1860.

His last name was adapted from his owners whom he had served lovingly all during his life. That family moved to Independence, Missouri, in the 1850s. The two sons, Cornelius and Chester Wentworth, took a hankering to go west with a wagon train. The train needed a cook, and Elijah, or Lige, as they called him, persuaded them to take him with them in that position. When he arrived in Denver, Lige loved the booming village.

In no time at all, he had endeared himself to most of the population of Denver. He would meet every new group of immigrants and welcome them to town, inviting them to settle in the wonderful territory of Colorado. His owners were not unhappy when emancipation freed the greying servant.

By the end of the War Between the States, Lige was able to obtain fees from hostelries in the area by greeting newcomers and suggesting where they might stay. Before long, he owned a bell, and would walk through town ringing it to advertise auctions and other sales. Elijah had a talent for poetry and would often give his messages in verse. His specialty was crying out the descriptions of lost children, horses, and pets.

Friends of Lige built him a small frame house on the east side of Seventeenth between Stout and California Streets.

Among his notable services, the old black man would call the alert for volunteer firemen when a blaze broke out, and he was considered a vital cog in the safety of the town. The volunteer firemen gave him a red shirt which he loved and would wear on special occasions.

When the first railroads arrived, he continued his meeting and greeting services.

Gradually his body grew a bit weary. Still, Elijah, who was a devout Christian, would hobble along the streets and give mini-sermons to passersby. He was given new clothes by a tailor, one of the fellow travelers on the wagon train for which he had cooked in 1860. Grocers and other businessmen kept him supplied with food and other necessities, and the local ladies aide society watched over him.

The city mourned his passing in 1880.

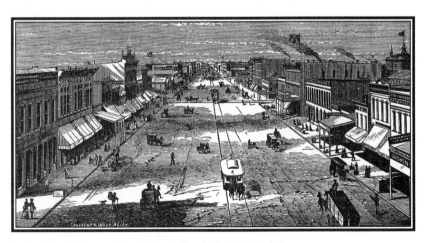

Larimer Street in Denver,. Colorado: Its Gold and Silver Mines *1879*

WHEN THE NAUGHTY NYMPHS
SHOCKED DENVER

But Thrilled Quite a Few People

Between Tremont Street and Court Place, and 15th and 16th Streets in downtown Denver once stood the majestic court house of Arapahoe County. In 1902 Denver became a city and county in its own right, and development of the civic center soon followed. When the old courthouse was demolished, the block became a pretty downtown park. Later it was the site of the May D&F department store, and now it is occupied by the Pavilions, a shopping center.

In the late 1890s two fountains graced the entrance to the court house. They were embellished with bronze statues of several naiads, beautiful women whose gowns showed above the knee. No one much cared until a spring morning when the commisisoners looked out and realized that there was not enough color in the fountain. This was, they believed, a state noted for its color, and those statues were rather drab.

As a result, they hired artists to paint the gowns of the ladies in bright colors, and the legs a flesh tone. When unveiled, they attracted many people to the grounds. Fountain spray was falling upon these inviting women. Workers in the building could not help spending time at the windows staring out at the maidens.

On the following Sunday, ministers and priests gave sermons condemning the outrageous décor, claiming it proved once and for all how the morality of Denverites had reached a heretofore never dreamed-of depth. Some merchants agreed that they were lascivious; some lawyers felt they would interfere with the dignity which would be afforded a house of law. On the other hand a number of so-called "men about town" thought the sparkling nymphs delightful.

After a few weeks of letters to editors, declamations, and protest banners, the paint was removed from the figures. As a later writer observed, this "surrealism in art" was too early for Denver.

THE COWTOWN OF COLORADO

Milkers of Denver

Despite the fact that the National Western Stock Show in Denver is one of the world's greatest such events, many Denverites have their hackles raised when their beloved city is called "an overgrown cow town." They are quick to point out with much justification the cultural attainments of the mile-high city.

It must be acknowledged, however, that a section of Denver was known as Cowtown less than a century ago. This includes the modern town of Glendale (encircled by the city of Denver) and on east to the Fairmount Cemetery. It embraced the area from Colorado Boulevard to Quebec Street, and between Alameda and Mississippi Avenues. George Washington High School and the vast Jewish Community Center are located in the former Cowtown. It was the center of the dairy industry which supplied the metropolitan area with milk, cheese, and other products from the 1880s through the first decades of the twentieth century.

Among the famous farms were the City Park Dairy, which boasted the largest producing herd in the Rocky Mountain region, Windsor Farms, Blue Ribbon, Stearns' Dairy, Carlson-Frink, Monarch, and many smaller operations.

In the earlier days before the automobile, the farmers would rise at 3:00 a.m. to begin the milking of the cows, and then process the milk, pouring it into cans. Then, with their wagons filled, they would reach the Denver homes before breakfast time. There the milkman would pour the milk into open pails at each customer's house.

It was reported that some of the horses that drew the wagons knew the route so well that they would move on and stop at the corner where the milkman would finish his block of deliveries. A resourceful horse from Windsor farm would lift the lids off garbage cans in the alleys, eating the discarded food at every stop. In later days, milk bottles made the process more sanitary, and motorized trucks afforded speedier service.

One horse-drawn milkman related that he had felt ill one Monday, but kept both milking and delivering all week. On Friday he was very sick. He went to the doctor and found out he had been doing all this work while he had typhoid fever!

Often people would leave notes to the milk carrier. George Jackson, who ran the routes from 1925 until 1968, remembered that he was sometimes asked to take the clothes off the clothesline, let the dog out, or lock the door. He was notified that there was something in the icebox for him, and at Christmas was asked in for a shot of whiskey. One year he received thirty-seven cartons of cigarettes as bonuses.

In 1981 Jack and Patricia Fletcher, former residents of Cowtown, wrote a booklet about its history, the source of much of this article. It wasn't published in Denver but in Yuma, Arizona.

"THE WORLD'S LEADING TRAFFIC ENGINEER"

Remembering the "Barnes Dance"

It was *Life* magazine that designated Henry Barnes "the world's leading traffic engineer" after this remarkable man, who had quit school at age fifteen, had established an entirely new system for urban traffic in America. Hank, as he liked to be called, was born in 1906 at Newark, New York, and went to work as a railroad section hand after finishing the eighth grade. Later he drove a bus to Florida on "the sucker run," selling people on buying land in that state's infamous real estate fiasco of the Twenties. After that he apprenticed as an electrician and made it to journeyman when he moved to Flint, Michigan, in 1926.

He became an auto worker and policeman there, but in 1931 an accident left him with a broken neck, a paralyzed arm, and a family to feed. His wife Hazel and their four children survived on what he could make building furniture and novelties of wood until, in 1938, he was made Flint's traffic signal engineer. In the meantime, he kept picking up courses in night school to learn about all phases of engineering. His success was outstanding; he was one of the rare individuals who, despite his lack of a college degree, received a year's fellowship to Yale School of Traffic Engineering. This led to his employment as Denver's traffic engineer in 1944.

Hank made bold changes to adjust the city to the era of heavy traffic: one-way streets, limited turns, and the famous "Barnes Dance" which halted all autos at downtown intersections while pedestrians could cross at all angles. By 1953 he had become famous and Baltimore hired him away from Denver. In the meantime he had developed computerized traffic lights which could keep traffic moving at steady speeds.

Then he went to New York City, site of the world's worst traffic jams, and set up programs which won worldwide fame. He found time to write an autobiography, **The Man With the Red and Green Eye**. Henry Barnes died of a heart attack in 1967 at the age of sixty-one.

Postcard of early Denver strret scene.   Courtesy of P. David Smith

DENVER HAD THE WORLD'S FIRST ELECTRIC TRAMWAY

Heavy Rains Posed a Problem

Denver had the first operating electric tramway in the world. It appeared on the Colorado Seminary campus, located at Fourteenth and Arapahoe, in 1885. It was the brainchild of Sydney Howe Short, Vice President and Chairman of the Physics Department at the Seminary, a secondary school which became the University of Denver the following year.

Short was born in 1838 in Ohio and made his way through several Eastern scientific schools before taking over the science department of the Denver school in 1880. He was enthralled by the power of electricity and built a circular track trolley on the campus which he christened the "John Henry." It worked with a middle "hot line" such as is used by modern subway systems; however, the danger of injury meant most of the line had to be buried, making it inefficient, especially in wet weather. However, Short expanded it with a line that ran up Colfax Avenue to Pennsylvania, across to Fifteenth Street, and then down to Center, a former downtown street. Heavy rains made the tramway inoperable, but the first thrust into a great idea had been made.

Short then moved to St. Louis where he tried again, encountering the same problems until he converted the electric supply to overhead wires. By that time alternating current had become practical.

He went on to develop a system for Cleveland, and then was called to London where he established the first trolley system to move by power other than horses. In his career he registered more than 500 patents. Short died in 1902 after an attack of appendicitis.

A SOUVENIR CIGAR BUTT AND A ROYAL HAIR

When Denver Swooned Over Grand Duke Alexis

In 1872 Denver was a young booming city with perhaps the most democratic attitudes of any place in the world. Nevertheless, when the son of Czar Alexander II, ruler of one of the world's most oppressive realms in history, came to town the Westerners felt so honored they staged the most impressive greeting they had ever given up to that time.

Grand Duke Alexis had received a great welcome by President Grant in Washington and came west to hunt buffalo with no less a master than William F. "Buffalo Bill" Cody, who could claim having laid to rest 4,280 bison. In spite of the fact that those animals were slow and very easy to shoot, the visiting royalty was only able to claim one buffalo in a hunt in Nebraska.

Following that failure, the tall, handsome Russian Romanoff heir arrived in Denver accompanied by General Phil Sheridan, head of the western division of the U.S. Army, and one of his most popular officers, George Armstrong Custer. Notified of the upcoming visit, former Governor John Evans and incumbent Governor Edward McCook had spared no expense to welcome the imperialist.

A banquet and ball were held at the American Hotel with 400 of Colorado's elite invited. The governor's wife, who had been ill, defied her doctor's orders to lead the Grand March with the Duke and then fainted in his arms.

Adorned with flags of Russia and the United States, the ballroom was magnificently transformed into what was believed to be a palatial venue for such nobility. Although the visitor was a poor dancer, every woman desired his accompaniment.

When the ball had ended, souvenirs were sought by many of Denver's upper crust. *The Rocky Mountain News* on January 19, 1872, reported the following treasures had been found: (Note to readers: the Denver daily newspapers often embellished stories even back in those days.) The stump of a cigar smoked by the Grand Duke had been rescued from a cuspidor. One woman preserved a tough piece of steak he had not eaten at the banquet. When the visitor trod on the train of her dress, another lady framed the torn fragment. Another preserved her satin shoe which had been stepped on by the royal boot. Still another had clipped a piece from the velvet upholstery of a chair upon which the great man had sat between dances. Then there was a royal hair stolen from the comb left in Alexis' room at the hotel.

During the ball a member of the orchestra mentioned to Custer that a large herd of buffalo was wintering near the town of Kit Carson. Plans were soon made, and Miguel Otero, the leading businessman of Kit Carson, arranged for a hunt there as the entourage left Denver.

Hunting was more successful at that town. A contingent of the army had been sent in from Kansas, and plenty of good whiskey and champagne were on hand. With everyone taking part in the hunt, more than 200 bison were slaughtered with the Russian nobleman killing a dozen by himself.

Upon his return to Europe, Alexis became a playboy for the most part, although he had symbolic responsibilities such as nominal head of the Russian Navy. He never married, but died in the arms of his mistress in Paris in 1908. He was fifty-eight years old. Only nine years later, the Russian Revolution succeeded and the Romanoff dynasty, which had ruled for hundreds of years, was annihilated.

Hunting buffalo from a train. London Illustrated News, *October 29, 1887*

WHY A DENVER STREET
KEPT GETTING RE-NAMED

From McGaa to Holladay to Market

William McGaa was one of the founders of Denver. He claimed to have run away from his London home as a youth seeking a seafaring life. Coming to the West in the Pike's Peak Gold Rush of 1858, he lived with the Arapahoe Indians where Cherry Creek joins the South Platte River.

Married to an Arapahoe woman, Wewatta, he was instrumental in naming some of the first streets in Denver. One of them he named for his wife, Wewatta, and another he named for himself.

The latter street would have remained McGaa, but it seems that William became something of a drunkard and would stroll around pointing out "his" street to newcomers. When the town fathers in 1866 decided to change the name of the street to Holladay, McGaa was infuriated and moved to the town of La Porte, Colorado. The next year he came back and went on a drinking binge. He was jailed. The next morning, he was found dead in his cell. It is said he died in a fit of delirium tremens.

Why the name change to Holladay? Ben Holladay was one of the most famous freighters to the region. His Central Overland, California and Pike's Peak Express had its terminal on the Denver side of Cherry Creek, thus giving Denver rather than Auroria, the mailing address. While his COC&PP Express usually did well, it had bad times. One of his drivers called it the "Clean Out of Cash and Poor Pay" line.

Noted observer Henry Villard wrote of Holladay that he was "illiterate, course, pretentious, boastful, false and cunning." Some Denverites agreed but granted that he had done much for the prosperity of the city.

As the years went by, Holladay Street became the most disreputable tenderloin in the West. It was there that many houses of ill repute, including those of Jenny Rogers and Mattie Silks, were to be found. It was also lined with gambling halls and saloons.

In 1877 the descendents of Holladay petitioned the city to remove their name from that notorious avenue. Two years later, Denver passed an ordinance naming it Market Street, perhaps because there was an open-air market nearby rather than, as some conjectured, a flesh market.

THE GREAT DENVER SQUIRREL WAR
Were Some Innocent Rodents Executed?

Historian Phil Goodstein included in his book **The Seamy Side of Denver** the nearly forgotten thirteen year edict by the City Council that created what some called a Squirrel-Shooting Squad in the police department.

A councilman in 1943 declared that squirrels in his district attacked bird nests and created other atrocities, such as making too much noise. He was able to get an ordinance passed for several districts that would declare any squirrel a public nuisance who engaged in such crimes.

Anyone seeing a squirrel doing wrong could call the police. There were protests that some of the rodents may not have been the offending creatures, but were killed without a fair trial.

Attempts were made to get Mayor Ben Stapleton to veto the law, but it remained on the books until 1956. How many well-behaed squirrels may have been shot during those days, along with the culprits?

It was about that time that the acclaimed graffic engineer, Henry Barnes, established mid-block traffic lights to control speed on one way streets. They were soon known as "squirrel crossings."

ABOUT THIS
AND THAT

A GRAVE MYSTERY IN SAGUACHE COUNTY

What Was Monk's Burden?

Near Colorado Highway 114, about seventeen miles west of the town of Saguache, there is an old fenced grave with a stone marker inscribed:

ARTHUR LLOYD MONK
MAJOR TO H M 22 FOOT
DIED APRIL 19, 1883
AGED 51 Yrs 7 Ms 18 Dys
"AND THE BURDEN LAID
UPON ME
WAS MORE THAN I COULD BEAR"

Why was he buried along what was at that time no more than a primitive wagon road? What was his burden? What was he doing out here in the West? The search for these answers is not yet complete and may never be. My search has turned up several possibilities but no proofs.

Gradually realizing that H.M. Foot 22 was a designation of infantry in British parlance, a check was made with the British Military Office, Department of Military Personnel Records. It was learned that there was indeed a man of this name who had served in the infantry back in the days of Queen Victoria. However, there were no specific dates available. The unit was the Twenty Second Foot Soldier Regiment.

Inquiries at nearby ranches yielded no information, and a search of the records of Saguache County was fruitless. An advertisement in the *Saguache Crescent* (the last newspaper in the state still to be published by the old letterpress method) did get one response, from Simon Halburian of that town.

He recalled a conversation with an old-timer who had since died, by the name of Glenn Coleman. Coleman related that Monk was a "black sheep" from an upper-class English family. The family engaged in a practice which has come to be known as remittance. A remittance man was one who received financial support to go to the American West as long as he promised not to return to England. There were a remarkable number of such beneficiaries in Colorado and Wyoming, many engaged in ranching.

A resident of Villa Grove in the San Luis Valley had heard a story that someone had run off with Monk's wife, and Arthur had died of grief.

A book written by Reverend William Worthington was published in 1930. It contained some reminiscences dating back as far as that era. The author, who was apparently a short man, claimed he could walk under the outstretched arms of several men including one Arthur Lloyd Monk. No further information on Monk was given.

Recently, Martha and Ed Quillen, publishers of *Colorado Central Magazine* in Salida, posted the puzzle on their website. Bruce Varcoe, of Kent, Washington, spotted the item, and believes that the grave is of a man who was married to one of his own ancestors and was in that regiment. Ann Cole Baker, Monk's wife, who was older than he, had died in 1874. Might that have been the burden?

There is a passage in the Bible, Galatians 6:5, which reads, "For every man shall bear his own burden." In some ways it seems that Arthur passed his onto those of us who are too curious.

The Sangre De Cristo Range as seen from Saguache. Courtesy of P. David Smith

THE BACA COUNTY FARMERS' REVOLUTION

When the Tractors Invaded Washington, D.C.

Although the town of Springfield could justifiably call itself the "Broomcorn Capital of the World" many years ago, farming in Baca County, in the southeastern corner of the state, has never been easy. It was among the hardest hit regions of the 1930s "Dust Bowl" and has to depend a great deal on deep wells for irrigation. The aquifer beneath the land has gradually lessened over the years.

Attempts to grow sugar beets, peanuts, and pinto beans have met with very little success, mainly due to poor climatic conditions. Wheat, milo maize, corn, and alfalfa are the primary crops.

During the latter part of the 1970s there was quite a demand for wheat to be sold to the Soviet Union. When the U.S. Congress set an embargo on wheat shipments to that nation, it resulted in serious financial difficulties to many wheat farmers.

Farmers Eugene Schroder and Alvin Jenkins who lived near the town of Campo, then formed leadership of the American Agricultural Movement. In 1978 they led hundreds of farmers from many wheat growing states who took their tractors and trucks to Washington, D.C. The vehicles paraded around the nation's capitol, creating quite a spectacle of protest to newspapers and television viewers throughout the nation.

One astute observer noted that the farmers may not have impressed Congress very much as they brought their finest and most expensive tractors for the parade. Had they used old tractors and trucks, it might have driven home the idea more effectively. A few adjustments were made to compensate the hard-hit wheat growers, but not enough to make up for the financial disaster faced by many, as farm foreclosures became all too frequent.

When the farm of Springfield's Jerry Wright was put up for Sheriff's auction January 4, 1983, some 250 farmers gathered in front of the County Court House to protest, "No Sale! No Sale!" They had come from a dozen states to revolt against what they regarded as unconstitutional land confiscation.

The gathering reached riot proportions, with a dozen deputies successfully holding off the mob with tear gas. The result was such as to split the people of Springfield into opposing camps for some time with boycotts of some businesses which did not support the methods of the American Agricultural Movement. Further to the extreme right were individuals who felt the AAM had not gone far enough in the uprising.

Things have pretty much settled down in the ensuing years, and the county has revived its proud tradition of individual determination in the face of adversity. Mass protest has given way to creative initiative in Baca County.

THE BACHELOR BULLS OF GRAND MESA

Wanted: At Least Fifty Cows!

High in the Plateau Valley beneath Grand Mesa in Western Colorado, people were just beginning to stake out their homesteads in 1882, a year after the removal of the Ute Indians to Utah. It was then that Milton Parker, from Washington, D.C., and his partner, Orson Adams, from New York City, decided that there was a great potential for big-time cattle raising. So it was that they bought fifty purebred registered bulls and brought them to grassland beneath the towering cliffs of the mesa. Their intention was to purchase cows for the bulls to start their enterprise. What they did not figure out was that the settlers did not wish to part with the few bovines with which they planned their own ranches and farms. The owners searched as far as Eastern Utah, but that region was just developing itself, and nary a cow could be bought.

Thus these dreamers were left with all those bulls and no cows. Historian Muriel Marshall has noted that it would take between 500 and 2,000 cows in order to break even in the growth of a cattle herd with that many bulls. Cowboys in the area began to joke about the enterprise, and soon they had named the stream which ran through the area "Bull Creek;" it flowed down from "Bull Lakes" and the ranch itself was named "Bull Basin," titles that still remain on the maps.

After two or three years of trying to satisfy the frustrated bulls, Parkers and Adams heard of Sinbad Valley in the extreme northwest corner of Montrose County. That region along the Dolores River was known as a hideout for cattle rustlers from Utah. Nearby is Sewemup Mesa where cattle brands were cut out and the hide sewed together again.

Thus it came to pass that the bulls were driven across the Gunnison and Dolores Rivers to Sinbad Valley. It is not known whether enough cows were for sale there or whether the bulls became tough steaks.

THE FAMOUS HORSE THEY CALLED ELIJAH

He Wintered Alone Above Timberline

"Bugs" was the name of a saddle horse who took tourists on rides in the summer and fall up into the mountains above the town of Buena Vista. According to historian Perry Eberhart, he had an "aversion to automobiles and women, especially women in slacks."

Whatever the reason, Bugs wandered away in the late fall of 1956 and was feared lost for good. The snows came and engulfed the 14,000-foot peaks west of Buena Vista, Mount Princeton and Mount Yale. In late December, an airplane spotted him struggling above timberline in the saddle between those peaks.

He instantly became a cause célébre, with newspapers all over the nation showing pictures of the stranded animal. The terrain in that rugged area made it practically impossible to reach him, so pilots decided to drop hay to him on a regular basis. These planes had to do some tricky maneuvers at that extremely high altitude noted for sudden downdrafts up on the top of the Continental Divide.

The press named him "Elijah." based on the biblical prophet who was kept alive by God sending ravens into the wilderness to save him from starvation. (I Kings: 17.) All winter long, reports were filed on the condition of the horse.

Passenger airplane flights between Denver and Gunnison flew over the saddle, a bit out of their regular route, just to point out the lonely animal. It has been said that Elijah's fate was noted in newspapers and radio broadcasts in London and Paris. Finally, the spring melt-off enabled a party of mountaineers to bring him down. He was then taken on a tour of Denver and other Colorado cities and towns so that everyone could celebrate his survival. They came, many of them women, in automobiles to view the acclaimed survivor. He had had his season of escape from all this and then was put back into service as the preferred mount on summer climbs of the mountains he knew so well.

THEY HEARD THE ANGELS SINGING

A Night to Remember

Rico, the mining town between Telluride and Dolores, was totally isolated by a massive snowstorm in January of 1952. Electricity, but not telephone service, was finally resumed between Rico and Dolores, yet slides had destroyed all services from Telluride. Both electrical and telephone repairmen were working on snowshoes, bending down, not climbing up, to reach the lines, so deep was that snow.

Ray Hauser and Royal Haulman were busy restoring the telephone wires from Telluride and had reached the summit of Lizard Head Pass when darkness overtook them. Rather than risk a dark hike through the avalanche route, they realized they would have to spend the night. The depot from the abandoned narrow-gauge railroad still stood atop the pass so they retreated into the rotting structure for whatever protection from the sub-zero winds it could afford.

They found a small stove in the building, and there were some old boards outside. Planks were broken up to fuel a fire, but the antique stove gave forth very little heat. An old lamp was found, and they lit it to keep some element of cheer in the depot.

As darkness enveloped the men, they began to feel ill. It seems the fumes from the lamp were nauseating them so it was extinguished, and to keep warm, they began to walk and jump around, and yelled at the former battery-operated telephone.

Ray couldn't remember exactly what they were shouting, but knew it was "appropriate to the occasion."

Returning from outside to get more wood for the stove, they heard, faintly, a female voice! This was it! The angels were already singing, calling for them! They looked around everywhere, even outside the building, but no one was there. The men about decided to attempt the perilous snowshoe trek back to their truck parked ten miles away.

They suddenly realized that the sounds were coming from the little megaphone into which they had been shouting. Drawing closer, they were able to make out the woman's voice. She was terrified.

It seems she was living in the abandoned depot at Rico, having redecorated the place as a home. Curtains had been hung over the "dead" telephone. Her husband was on the night shift at a mine, and alone with her children, she began to hear voices. The frozen bodies of two postal carriers who had been caught in a slide had just been brought in on toboggans and left near the old depot, now her home, to await proper disposal. She imagined that the ghosts of those unfortunates were calling. Then came her realization that it was the telephone talking: the battery still functioned!

The "phantom lady" asked the repairmen to call back via Telluride to Cortez where a hearse could be brought up when the road to Rico was opened.

When dawn crept in after a very long night, the men were able to resume their duties, finally meeting repairmen from the direction of Rico and being taken to Dolores for some needed sleep.

It was twenty-five years later when Ray and his wife were once again on Lizard Head Pass looking at a herd of deer. Another car was parked at the site where the depot had once stood. Ray told of his adventure to Edgar Branson, the driver of the other car. Suddenly, Branson called to his wife, waiting in the car.

She was the "phantom lady" with whom the telephone men had visited that fateful night in 1952. She explained that the same night, a young couple who had been stranded sought shelter in her depot-home. The wife was expecting a baby at any moment, and Mrs. Branson feared she would have to be a midwife in addition to all the other upsets.

Ray reflected that on that cold night their "angel" had probably had more an ordeal than he and his partner.

SOME LITTLE THINGS I DIDN'T KNOW

Including Some Serendipities

Cy Warman was the famous editor who wrote the lines "Where it's day all day in the daytime / and there is no night in Creede." He later wrote for a newspaper in Denver, and then went east, where he wrote one of the most popular songs of the 1880's, "Sweet Marie." From that work he became wealthy for the first time - so much so that his wife, for whom he had written the song, divorced him and was awarded alimony of $125 a month.

Joes, Colorado, was probably named that because three men who were named Joe lived there at the time of its founding. Another source claims there was a business there named Joe's Ice Cream Parlor.

At Kremmling, there is an annual dog sled race named "Ididarace."

The observation tower at Genoa was built along old Highway 24 before I-70 bypassed the town, but the structure is still open to the public. It is claimed that a person can view Wyoming, South Dakota, Nebraska, Kansas, New Mexico, and Colorado from the tower. However one has to doubt the claim by the curator of the museum there that one can see the Teton Range of Wyoming from the viewing platform.

Town Pump at Iliff. Photo by Author

At Paonia, the Land's End Foundry is one the most popular places for casting statues anywhere in the nation. The largest bronze statue in America was made there for Fort Lauderdale, Florida: a giant porpoise.

Possibly the only place in Colorado which still has a town pump remaining is at Iliff. The pump has been preserved at the center of the crossroads downtown.

Nucla has a statue of a prairie dog in its park. This was the site of the Top Gun Prairie Dog Shoot for several years.

Observation tower at Genoa. Photo by author

Protesters came from far away to try to stop the killing of the little animals that are a bane to ranchers. If they had been called what they are, "prairie rats," there might not have been any complaints.

Calhan, near Colorado Springs, claims to have the highest elevation of any non-mountain town in Colorado at 6,507 feet above sea level.

The last letterpress-printed newspaper in Colorado is the *Saguache Crescent.* It makes good use of its linotype. Incidentally, at Saguache one can also see a sign on the window of a former pharmacy which reads "Drug Dealer."

With a population of only around 200, Sedgwick may be the smallest place anywhere in Colorado to have a Buddhist temple.

The settlement known as Firstview on U.S. 40 between Cheyenne Wells and Kit Carson was originally a station established by the Kansas Pacific Railway in 1904. At that time one coming from the east could get the first sight of Pike's Peak, but only rarely is the air that clear today.

There is a gasoline station from the 1930s in Holyoke, completely preserved by the Phillips County Historical Society.

At Manassa, the birthplace of the famous world heavyweight boxing champion Jack Dempsey, there is an entire museum devoted to the life and career of the man the press used to refer to as the "Manassa Mauler."

The first long-distance telephone line in Colorado was built in 1889 over Mosquito Pass, the state's highest at 13,186 feet elevation. It connected Leadville with Denver. This was only the seventeenth such system in the world.

Prairie dog at Nucla. Photo by author

It is very probable that the town of Deer Trail in Arapahoe County held the first rodeo with strict rules in the United States. It was called a bronco busting contest and took place July 4, 1869.

At 4:30 p.m. on Sunday, July 6, 1924 a meteorite fell in 27 or more pieces near the town of Johnstown, creating a sonic boom and leaving a trail of vapor. At a nearby cemetery, a funeral service was in progress when a large chunk fell within 200 feet of the grave. The undertaker dug up the fragment and took it to town, where a baseball game was in progress. As the fans had all heard the noise, they flocked to see the visitor from outer space and paid little attention to the rest of the game. That specimen is a center of attraction at the Denver Museum of Natural History where it launched a continuing study of meteorites.

Gas Station at Holyoke. Photo by author

ACKNOWLEDGMENTS

The writer wishes to express his gratitude to the following individuals, libraries, and institutions who have helped a great deal in the preparation of this work:

Dave Fishell, Debbie Kovisec, Jamie Hamilton, Ron Lambetta, and Joan Young, all of Grand Junction.

Linda Powers, La Junta; Jeanne Beckly, Glenwood Springs; Beth Pelton and Alice Benge, Cheyenne Wells; Jane Burns and Adolph "Dutch" Johnson, Kit Carson; Robert Faitzler, Flagler; Jerry Chubbick, Ovid; Tommy Pierce, Fruita; Maureen Keller, Golden; Ken Reyher, Olathe; Ellen Thrasher, Sterling; Father Gallagher, Avondale; Gary Hanna, Springfield; Martha and Ed Quillen, Salida, Charmaine Ness, Deer Trail; Sue Cohn of Leadville, and Bruce Varcoe, of Kent, Washington.

Libraries and institutions include Baca County Library, Springfield; Deer Trail's Davies Library; Trinidad Public Library; Lamar Public Library; Bent County Library and Kit Carson Museum, Las Animas; Grand County Museum, Hot Sulphur Springs; Cheyenne Wells Museum; Kit Carson Museum; Northeastern Junior College, Sterling; Springfield Library and Chamber of Commerce; Logan County Chamber of Commerce, Sterling; and the Mesa County Library, Grand Junction.

He is very indebted to his wife, Joan, for helping so much in research and in reading the manuscript, and to Marisa and Collin Fay in Palisade; to Randy Fay, Nancy Lewis-Lentz and John McGuire in Denver, Jack Murphy, Denver, Troy Mellon, Johnstown and to Dede Fay and David Batura in Granby.

BIBLIOGRAPHY

Arnold, Frazer. "Samuel Hartsel, Pioneer Cattleman." *Colorado Magazine.* May, 1942.

Arvada Historical Society. *Arvada, Just Between You and Me.* Boulder, 1985.

Ashback-Sladek, Ron D. "Hollywood in the Rockies." *Colorado Heritage.* 1986, No. 2.

Athearn, Robert G. *The Coloradans.* Albuquerque, NM, 1976.

Benson, Jack A. "Before Skiing Was Fun." *The Western Historical Quarterly.* Oct., 1977.

Benson, Maxine. *1001 Colorado Place Names.* Lawrence, KS, 1994.

Bent County History Book Committee. *Bent County (Colorado) History.* Las Animas, 1986-7.

Blair, Edward, and E. Richard Churchill. *Everybody Came to Leadville.* Leadville, 1971.

Blair, Edward. *Leadville, Colorado's Magic City.* Boulder, 1980.

Block, Augusta. "Old Lige." *Colorado Magazine.* July, 1942.

Blue, Daniel. *Thrilling Narrative of the Adventures, Sufferings and Starvation of Pike's Peak Gold Seekers on the Plains of the West in the Winter and Spring of 1859.* Whiteside County, IL, 1860 (Reprint: Fairfield, NH, 1968).

Brown, Seletha A. "Eliza Buford Rothrock, Colorado Pioneer." *Colorado Magazine.* Sept. 1946.

Bueler. *Roof of the Rockies.* Evergreen, 1986.

Campbell, Rosemae W. *From Trappers to Tourists: Fremont County, Colorado 1830 - 1950.* Palmer Lake, 1972.

Carter, Harvey L. "The Curious Case of the Slandered Scout, the Aggressive Anthropologist, the Delinquent Dean and the Acquiescent Army." *Denver Westerners Brand Book.* 1972.

Cassells, E. Steve. *The Archaeology of Colorado.* Boulder, 1983.

Chickering, Sharon K. "Twin Lakes Tragedy." Colorado Central (Salida). Jan. 2000.

Coca, Ray. "Baseball Greats Made History at GJ Field." *Newcomers Magazine* (Grand Junction). Spring, 1999.

Collins, Dabney Otis. *Land of Tall Skies.* Colorado Springs, 1977.

Collins, Dabney Otis. *The Hanging of Bad Jack Slade.* Denver, 1966.

Cooper, Ray. "Interesting Bits of History." *Colorado Magazine.* March, 1946.

Crum, Sally. *People of the Red Earth.* Santa Fe, NM, 1996.

Cuba, Stanley L., "Poles in the Early Musical and Theatrical Life of Colorado." *Colorado Magazine.* Summer, 1977.

Cumpston, Lori. "Chicken Crooner." *Grand Junction Daily Sentinel.* Sept. 2, 1999.

Daniels, Bettie, and Virginia McConnell. *The Springs of Manitou*. Denver, 1964.

Denver Catholic Register. May 31, 1934.

Denver Post. April 5, 1972.

Denver Post. "Old Wall Must Go." June 25, 1899.

Denver Westerners Monthly Roundup. April, 1967.

Donachy, Patrick L. *Echoes of Yesterday, Vol. II*. Trinidad, 1983.

Durrell, Glen R. "Homesteading in Colorado." *Colorado Magazine*, Spring, 1974.

Eberhart, Perry. *Ghosts of the Colorado Plains*. Athens, OH, 1986.

Eberhart, Perry. *Guide to the Colorado Ghost Towns and Mining Camps*. Denver, 1959.

Eberhart, Perry. *Treasure Tales of the Rockies*. Denver, 1961.

Ellis, Amanda M. *The Strange, Uncertain Years*. Hamden, CT, 1959.

Emrich, Duncan. *It's an Old Wild West Custom*. Kingswood, Surrey, England, 1951.

Encyclopedia Britannica. 11th Edition: "Paderewski."

Even, David. *All the Years of American Popular Music*. New York, 1979.

Everett, George, and Wendell F. Hutchinson. *Under the Angel of Shavano*. Denver, 1963.

Fales, E.D. Jr. "Terror at Twin Lakes." *Popular Science*. Feb., 1963.

Fay, Abbott. *Famous Coloradans*. Paonia, 1990.

Fay, Abbott. *I Never Knew That About Colorado*. Ouray, 1997.

Fay, Abbott. *Mountain Academia: A History of Western State College of Colorado*. Boulder, 1968.

Fay, Abbott. *Ski Tracks in the Rockies: A Century of Colorado Skiing*. Evergreen, 1984.

Freitz, Leland. "World's Largest Producer of Advertising Films: The Alexander Film Company." *Denver Westerners Brand Book*, 1972.

Ferril, Thomas Hornsby. *I Hate Thursday*. New York, 1946.

Flagler News. Sept. – Oct. Editions, 1950.

Fletcher, Jack and Patricia. *Denver Cowtown*. Yuma, AZ, 1981.

Fautz, Dell R. *Geology of Colorado Illustrated*. Grand Junction, 1994.

Fowler, Gene. *A Solo in Tom-Toms*. New York, 1931.

Fuller, Leon W. "Governor Waite and His Silver Panacea." *Colorado Magazine*. March 1933.

Goodstein, Phil. *Denver Streets*. Denver, 1994.

Goodstein, Phil. *The Seamy Side of Denver*. Denver, 1993.

Goodstein, Phil. "Monumental Denver." *Colorado Heritage, 1987, Issue 3*.

Grand Junction Daily Sentinel. Sept. 13, 1994.

Gregg, Gilbert E. *Incidentally: Anecdotes from The History of an Earlier Day in Buena Vista, Colorado.* Salida, 1975.

Gresham, Hazel. *North Park.* Walden, 1975.

Gunnison School Board Bus Crash Hearings, 1971-2.

Hauser, Ray. *Rico, Colorado: Winter, 1951-52.* Unpublished Manuscript. Montrose, 1978.

Helmers, Dow. *Tragedy at Eden.* Pueblo, 1971.

Higgens, Frances. "'Sniktau' Pioneer Journalist." *Colorado Magazine.* June, 1928.

Jones, William C. and Elizabeth B. *Buckwalter: The Colorado Scenes of a Pioneer Photojournalist, 1890-1920.* Boulder, 1989.

Kautz, Susan. "Wood Sculptures Pop Up All Over Town" in Wells, Bud. (Ed.). *Logan County: Better by 100 Years.* Dallas, 1987.

Keener, James and Christine. Colorado 141: *Unaweep to Uravan.* Grand Junction, 1988.

Kelly, Jack. *Koshare.* La Junta, 1985.

Kirk, Andy (as told to Amy Lee). *Twenty Years on Wheels.* Ann Arbor, MI, 1989.

Kittle, J. Leslie. "An Authentic Form of Folk Music in Colorado." *Colorado Magazine.* March, 1945.

Lamar Daily News. Aug. 15, 1957.

Leadville Chronicle, July 10, 1880.

Leadville Chronicle, Aug. 2, 1880.

Leadville Herald-Democrat. Jan. 22, 1962.

Leadville Herald-Democrat. Jan., 10, 1967.

Lecompte, Janet. *Pueblo, Hardscrabble, Greenhorn: The Upper Arkansas, 1832 - 1856.* Norman, OK, 1978.

Leonard, Stephen J. *Trials and Triumphs: A Colorado Portrait of the Great Depression.,* Niwot, 1993.

Life. Oct. 22, 1945.

Linscome, Sanford A. "Henry Houseley, Versatile Musician of Early Denver." *Colorado Magazine.* Winter, 1972.

Locke, Raymond. *The Book of the Navajo.* Los Angeles, CA, 1992.

Look, Al. *Sidelights on Colorado.* Denver, 1967.

Marshall, Muriel. *Island in the Sky: The Story of Grand Mesa.* Ouray, 1999.

McElvin, Walt. Letter to Don Washburn (Re: Wildwood Lodge), in *The Historian.* March, 2000.

McCraw, L.R. *Mountain Tales, Faded Fables and Hi-Jinks."* Gunnison, 1991.

McGue, D.B. "John Taylor - Slave-born Colorado Pioneer." *Colorado Magazine.* Sept., 1941.

Melrose, Frances. *Rocky Mountain Memories*. Denver, 1986.

Miller, Max, and Fred Mazzula. *Holladay Street*. New York, 1962.

Mines Magazine. Golden. July-Aug., Nov.-Dec., 1999.

Murphy, Jack.. "Air Mail Express: Meteorites in the Museum" in *Museum Quarterly*, Denver Museum of Natural History, Winter, 1999.

Nelson, Jim. *Glenwood Springs: The History of a Rocky Mountain Resort*. Ouray, 1999.

Newsweek. Jan. 17, 1983.

Noel, Thomas, Paul Mahoney, and Richard Stevens. *Historical Atlas of Colorado*. Norman, OK, 1994.

O'Neal, Bill. *Encyclopedia of Western Gunfighters*. Norman, OK, 1979.

O'Steen, Ike. *A Place Called Baca*. Springfield, 1979.

Owens, Sister M. Lilliana. "Christ of the Rockies." *Colorado Magazine*. May, 1941.

Parkhill, Forbes. *The Wildest of the West*. Denver, 1957.

Paxson, Frederic L. *The Last American Frontier*. New York, 1910.

Payne, Stephen. *Where the Rockies Ride Herd*. Denver, 1965.

Probst, Nell Brown. *Uncommon Men and the Colorado Prairie*. Caldwell, ID, 1992.

Reddin, Paul. *Wild West Shows*. Urbana, IL, 1999.

Reyher, Bill. *History of Lamar and Wiley, Colorado*. Lamar, 1968.

Reyher, Wilbur. *Scrapbook*. Lamar.

Rist, Martin. "A Fake that Rocked the World." *Denver Westerners Brand Book*, 1970.

Rizzari, Francis B. *Colorado's Underground Inferno*. Denver Westerners Roundup. April, 1968.

Rockwell, Wilson. *The Utes, A Forgotten People*. Denver, 1964.

Rocky Mountain News. June 12, 1902.

Rocky Mountain News. April 18 & 23, 1893.

Rocky Mountain News. Oct. 2, 1950.

Rocky Mountain News. Jan. 19, 1872.

Rocky Mountain News. Jan. 4 & 16, 1983.

Rocky Mountain News. December 1956 and June 1957.

Rollins, John Q. Jr. "John Q.A. Rowlins, Colorado Builder." *Colorado Magazine*. May, 1939.

Secrest, Clark. "The Junk Lane Gang's Great Disappointment." *Colorado Heritage*. Spring, 1992.

Secrest, Clark. "The Colorado State Liar." *Colorado Heritage*. Autumn, 1993.

Secrest, Clark. "Follow That Story." *Colorado Heritage*. Spring, 1998.

Secrest, Clark. "Private First Class Dale H. Maple." *Colorado Heritage*, Winter, 1995.

Secrest, Clark. "No Right to be Poor." *Colorado Heritage*. Winter, 1998.

Shaw, Luella. *True History of Some of the Pioneers of Colorado*. Hotchkiss, 1909.

Shoemaker, Len. *Saga of a Forest Ranger*. Boulder, 1958.

Smith, Duane A. *Silver Saga: The Story of Caribou, Colorado*. Boulder, 1974.

Smith, Duane. "Mighty Casey Matches the Mountains: The Origins of Baseball in Colorado." *Colorado Heritage*. Spring, 1995.

Sprague, Marshall. *"Healers in Pike's Peak History."* Denver Westerners Roundup. Dec., 1967.

Sprague, Marshall. *A Gallery of Dudes*. Lincoln, NE, 1966.

Taylor, Morris F. *Trinidad, Colorado Territory*. Trinidad, 1966.

Taylor, Ralph C. *Colorado South of the Border*. Denver, 1963.

Teal, Roleta, and Betty Lee Jacobs. *Kiowa County*. Eads, 1976.

Templeton, Sardis. *The Lame Captain*. Los Angeles, CA, 1965.

Thrapp, Dan L. *Encyclopedia of Frontier Biography, Vol. III*. Glendale, CA, 1988.

Time Almanac 2000.

Turk, Gayle. *Wet Mountain Valley*. Colorado Springs, 1975.

Twain, Mark. *Roughing It*. Hartford, CT, 1872.

Villard, Henry. *The Past and Present of the Pike's Peak Gold Regions*. St. Louis, MO, 1860.

Vroom, Peter D. "When Surrealism Stunned Denver." *Colorado Magazine*. Sept. 1946.

Weigle, Marta. *Brothers of the Light, Brothers of the Blood: The Penitentes of the Southwest."* Albuquerque, NM, 1976.

Whiteside, James. *Colorado: A Sports History*. Niwot, 1999.

Wolle, Muriel Sibell. *Stampede to Timberline*. Boulder, 1949.

Worrall, Janet E. "Prisoners on the Home Front." *Colorado Heritage*, 1990 No. 1.

Worthington, William. *In the Sunny San Luis*. Providence, RI, 1930.

WPA Federal Writers Project. *Colorado: A Guide to the Highest State*. New York, 1941.

Zuck, David. *Cheyenne County, Colorado Trails & Stage Stations*. Cheyenne Wells, ND.

INDEX